Endorsements

Xavier Williams, Telecom Executive

"Trudy has really captured something special here. To remind and reinforce that we can lead from wherever we are is an essential lesson for all of us. As the global marketplace continues to evolve, understanding and embracing EQUALITY will be essential for all leaders!"

Mark King, Global Head, Diversity & Inclusion, Kellogg Company

"Congratulations Trudy on writing what I believe will be a game changing book. I have seen these principles that you write about in action and know that they work. Those truly serious about moving the needle on diversity and inclusion will greatly benefit from this book. Your example of courageous leadership is inspiring!"

Kim Smith, Former Executive, Texas Instruments

"It takes true courage to go first. Whether you are the first woman or the first person of color to pursue careers where men have dominated, your voice matters. It did for me. As one of the first females to publicly champion women in STEM, I personally know that change is challenging. But I also know that what Trudy recommends in building partnerships across differences is the secret sauce to success. Congratulations!"

D0778351

James White, Former Chairman, President and CEO Jamba Juice, Board Member

"Trudy has always been the truth teller! Her passion to drive equality is contagious. She has masterfully addressed the issues that make people uncomfortable in a way that draws you in. I join Trudy in using my voice to drive equality. It is more important now than ever before. Well done!"

Alison Kenney Paul, Principal | Retail & Distribution, Deloitte

"Trudy is convincing in her position that one leader's voice can make a difference. If you listen to Trudy's arguments for change and embrace personal responsibility to leave the business world better than you found it – change will happen. I am happy to be able to make the pledge and join the movement. This is a must-read book for any leader who wants to succeed. Awesome work!"

Julie Hamilton, Senior Vice President, Chief Customer and Commercial Leadership Officer, The Coca-Cola Company

"Reading EQUALITY is a great reminder that there's never been a better time for women in the business world than now. This book is compelling and stirs your heart in a way that motivates you to use your voice as a female leader to take the lead in creating a diversity and inclusion breakthrough. EQUALITY is an inspiring read!"

Bonnie Hill, Co-founder, Icon Blue, Inc. Board Member
"The stories in this book remind us all that one voice can be the catalyst for advancing change but it also reminds us that transformation only happens in community. It is time for us to come together across differences and make this world a better place. If not for our generation for the generation that we will leave it to. Thanks for offering all of us a roadmap to a better future!"

Tara Mohr, author of *Playing Big: Practical Wisdom for Women Who Want to Speak Up, Create and Lead*
"I'm thrilled that Trudy Bourgeois has created this thoughtful resource to inspire all of us to be better advocates, allies, and change-makers around diversity and equality in the corporate sphere. This book is inspiring, informative, and highly practical. Thank you Trudy, for stepping into your own leadership and playing big in writing it."

Kellie McElhaney PhD, Associate Adjunct Professor, UC Berkeley-Haas School of Business
"Finally a book comes forth that reminds women of their true power and voice to advance change. Trudy is spot on in her assertion that business sustainability goes hand in hand with diversity and inclusion. What company wouldn't want to build a workforce that mirrors the face of their consumers? It's the only way to drive true innovation."

Mike Solomita, VP, Advanced Services, US Public Sector at Cisco

"The journey to a business world where we fully capitalize on our diversity starts with the leader. We need to make it crystal clear that our differences are assets, and that it is safe for all to share their voices. That is how we gain an accurate understanding of reality and can then make better informed decisions and execute. Thank you, Trudy, for the call to the dominant group to step up!"

Equality: Courageous Conversations About Women, Men, and Race to Spark a Diversity and Inclusion Breakthrough

Equality: Courageous Conversations About Women, Men, and Race to Spark a Diversity and Inclusion Breakthrough

Trudy Bourgeois

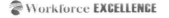

The Center for Workforce Excellence, Publisher
Dallas, TX

Printed in the United States of America
ISBN-13: 9781976596339
ISBN-10: 1976596335

Dedication

I would like to dedicate this book to all the men and women who paved the way for equality to help us get to where we are today. And to all the men and women who will use their voice to engage in courageous conversations to move the needle closer to true equality in the future.

May history mark our contributions in a way that reflects our heartfelt commitment to the belief that all people are created equal and deserve equal opportunities for success!

Contents

Foreword

After a rich and rigorous conversation about race, gender, and diversity and inclusion in my office in New York, I knew I'd found a kindred spirit in Trudy Bourgeois. A research partner of ours—a large technology company—wanted our expertise as they accelerated their commitment to diversity and inclusion. This time around they wanted more than to move the needle, they wanted a major breakthrough. Trudy's passion filled the room as she talked about unleashing talent across the divides of difference. As she began to dig deeper into systemic barriers related to bias, ethnicity, and privilege, I understood how impressive she was —the "real deal" in terms of authenticity as well as subject matter expertise. Her words resonated with my own long-standing commitment to fully realizing human potential across the divides of gender, race and class.

As an economist and social entrepreneur, I have explored these subjects for decades and appreciate

Trudy's discerning eye and engaging style. As a fellow author, I wanted to better understand her drive to tackle these subjects – typically the last conversation employers or employees want to have. Countless research studies, some from my own organization, document the pervasive nature of bias and discrimination as well as the profound discomfort around addressing such issues.

[1]Despite what many of us see as the long road ahead to equality, there are those who insist that we've left those outdated ism's behind, and that there's nothing left to fight for. Well, there certainly is. Racial anxieties remain pervasive, and injustice persists, embedded into our institutions and collective subconscious.

These issues demand our unwavering attention and scrutiny, and Trudy has her finger on the pulse with what she calls "courageous conversations." In this book she calls on us to reflect on our beliefs and provides tools and tactics that allow us to get outside our comfort zone. Few writers both challenge readers and guide them in such practical ways and I encourage you to consider deeply every tough question Trudy asks and every concrete action she presents. Perhaps you will find yourself in the

---

1 See: Ella Bell Smith, Sylvia Ann Hewlett, Trevor Phillips, and Ripa Rashid, with Melinda Marshall and Tai Wingfield, *Easing Racial Tensions at Work* (New York: Center for Talent Innovation, 2017); Larry Shannon-Missal, "Gender Equality in the Workforce: The United States Has Come a Long Way, but Barriers Remain," *Harris Poll*, March 3, 2016, http://www.theharrispoll.com/business/Workforce-Gender-Equality.html

stories contained in this book and discover that the words of a stranger reflect your own experiences. I hope the stirring narratives Trudy has collected not only shift your perspective on difference but also inspire you to raise your own voice and help champion the causes of open honest exchange and true inclusion.

As a mother and now a grandmother, I want a world where my grandchildren (who are wonderfully diverse) are welcomed and valued for who they are and what they can contribute, in the workplace and elsewhere. It is a wish that many of us share. I hope you accept the invitation that that this book extends to join a movement dedicated to creating a workplace where everyone can flourish. There is no better legacy.

-Sylvia Ann Hewlett

Acknowledgements

The process of writing a book is truly a labor of love. My first two books stirred my heart. I discovered so much about who I wanted to be as a leader. My hope was to inspire others to reflect on their leadership impact.

This book is about change. It is a subject with great meaning and great possibilities for national if not global change. I have had the fortune of so many people helping me with this project over the last two years. From the woman who manages my life and squeezed out 30 minutes here and there to give me time to write the book, Karen Best, to the initial editor, Jenny Claggett, to the production editor, Laura Gloege, to the final book editor, Lisa Lopez. It has truly been a collaborative experience.

I am so grateful to all the leaders who allowed me to interview them. Some names have been changed to protect the innocent and the guilty. But all of their stories will move you to a point of emotional buy-in for driving equality. I believe that is what it will take to truly spark a diversity and inclusion breakthrough. It is going to take leaders who have the courage to talk about subjects that for decades have been considered taboo, like race in the workplace. Please know that your experiences have and will continue to have impact for generations to come.

I am always appreciative of my family. My husband, Mike, who has patiently listened to me complain about the way women and people of color are treated day after day. My daughter, MaryEllen, who in her own way is leading equality by sowing positive seeds of understanding into the hearts of the boys and girls that she teaches at the first-grade level. Her husband, Ryan, my new son-in-law, who was a real help and champion. There is a story in the book about him that makes me cry in a good way every time that I read it. As my husband puts it, "He is a father's dream of a son-in-law." To my first born, Adam, who was born with down syndrome. Thank you for the gift of you. I will always fight for your rights until the day I die.

I want to extend my heartfelt thanks to all the women and men who are paving the way day in and day out to snuff out injustices and drive equality. You inspire me to want to do more. You make me believe in possibilities. I am especially grateful to Sylvia Ann Hewlett for writing the foreword. I am forever grateful.

Finally, I want to thank each person that reads this book who will dig deep to pave the way for a future where men and women, no matter what background, ethnicity or other difference can be afforded equal opportunities to experience success. That's what I want for my children and the grandchildren that I hope God will bless us to see. I believe that deep down we all want equal opportunities. We all want to be accepted. We all want to belong. We all want to be treated fairly. One day all of our careers will end. Trust me, people won't remember how many widgets you sold, nor how many spreadsheets that you created. They might not even remember how many products you actually were responsible for creating, but they WILL remember how you treated them. Thank you for digging deep and making the pledge to do the work!

Introduction

Insanity. It's a word that is used in many different ways. One definition that has frequently been used throughout history is this: "Madness, the non-legal word for insanity." Another definition we often hear is: "Doing the same thing and expecting different results."

For the purposes of setting the context for this book, we will use the latter. Why? The business world has been applying the same techniques and strategies to support the advancement of women and people of color for decades and getting the same results. Diversity and inclusion have been positioned as a *business imperative*, but it is clear that most business leaders do not understand the notion of the word "imperative."

Thus, the word insanity comes to mind — doing the same thing repeatedly and expecting different results.

According to the World Economic Forum report from 2016, gender equality in general is going backwards. The report finds that progress towards parity in the key

economic pillar has slowed dramatically with the gap —
which stands at 59% — now larger than at any point since
2008. The key areas measured included Educational
Attainment, Health and Survival, Economic Opportunity
and Political Empowerment. In 2015, projections based on
the Global Gender Gap Report data suggested that the
economic gap could be closed within 118 years, or 2133.[2]

While the report offers little in the way of new expla-
nations or solutions, it's worth noting for its efforts to call
out not just the leadership gap between men and women,
but between white women and minority women at the
top. "A lot of the leadership research is about all women,"
says Catherine Hill, AAUW's vice president of research.
"I think the stories about black and Hispanic women and
other minorities get shadowed."[3]

The AAUW report visualizes this striking divide in
one staggering chart, using 2014 data from the Equal
Employment Opportunity Commission to illustrate how
men and women of different racial and ethnic groups
are represented in both the private sector workforce as a
whole and in its senior-level executive jobs. One can just

2 World Economic Forum, *Gender Equality Is Sliding Backwards, Finds Our Global Report*, 2016, https://www.weforum.org/agenda/2016/10/gender-gap-report-2016-equality-sliding-backwards/.
3 Jena McGregor, "This Staggering Chart Shows How Few Minority Women Hold Executive Positions," *Washington Post* (Washington, D.C.), March 30, 2016. https://www.washingtonpost.com/news/on-leadership/wp/2016/03/30/this-staggering-chart-shows-how-few-minority-women-hold-executive-positions/?utm_term=.51fca2483cbc.

make out the 1.3 percent of executives that are Hispanic women (who comprise 6.2 percent of the private sector workforce). Or the 1.5 percent of executives who are African-American women (7.6 percent of the private sector workforce).[4]

I was sitting with a group of thought leaders recently, and the question came up as to whether progress had been made in the advancement of women of color. When it was my turn to comment, I simply stated, "White women have been the biggest beneficiary of affirmative action, while the numbers for women of color are going backwards."

"Really? the group responded.

"Really," I said.

In the high-profile case of Abigail Fisher vs. the University of Texas – Austin, the U.S. Supreme Court ruled 4-3 in favor of the University of Texas. This decision essentially allowed affirmative action to survive another day saying that the university's consideration of race in admission is legal. In case you're not familiar with this case, Abigail Fisher was denied admission to the University of Texas, according to her lawsuit, because she is white.[5] According to a *Time* magazine article, Fisher framed her college rejection as reverse racism, but studies show that

---

4 Ibid.

5 Kaitlin Mulhere, "Supreme Court Says Using Race in Admissions Decisions Is Fair Game," *Time* (New York, NY), June 23, 2016. http://time.com/money/4379905/affirmative-action-upheld-fisher-v-university-of-texas-austin/.

affirmative action actually favors white women like the plaintiff, not minorities.[6]

Let me offer some context. Affirmative action, when it was introduced by President John F. Kennedy in 1961, originally required entities that receive federal funding to take tangible steps "to ensure that applicants are employed and that employees are treated during employment without regard to their race, creed, color, or national origin." In 1967, Lyndon Johnson added sex to that list.[7]

According to one study in 1995, six million women, the majority of whom were white, had jobs they wouldn't have otherwise held but for affirmative action.[8] Research from LeanIn.Org and McKinsey & Co. suggests that women of color are the most underrepresented group in the upper ranks of companies, and their numbers drop steeply at the middle and senior levels. Women of color make up 12% of first-level managers, compared with 45% for their white male peers. At the C-suite level, women of color

6 Kaitlin Mulhere, "How Wednesday's Supreme Court Case Could Change Colle Affirmative Action," *Time* (New York, NY), December 8, 2015. http://time.com/money/4140410/preview-fisher-texas-supreme-court-affirmative-action/.

7 Chloe Angyal, "Affirmative Action Is Great For White Women. So Why Do They Hate It?," *Huffington Post*, (New York, NY), January 21, 2016, updated June 23, 2016. http://www.huffingtonpost.com/entry/affirmative-action-white-women_us_56a0ef6ae4b0d8cc1098d3a5.

8 Tim Wise, "Is Sisterhood Conditional?: White Women and the Rollback of Affirmative Action," *Timwise.org*, September 23, 1998. http://www.timwise.org/1998/09/is-sisterhood-conditional-white-women-and-the-rollback-of-affirmative-action/.

make up just 3% of the workforce, compared with 71% for white men.[9]

My response generated two more questions: Do you think diversity and inclusion are a viable business imperative? And are we better than we were 20 years ago? I would have to say we are, but I *don't* believe diversity and inclusion are viable business imperatives.

As further explanation, I continued. "As a former senior sales and marketing executive, I have a bias about getting results. Business leaders are paid to get results. They are responsible for every part of the business including people, performance and profits. If a top customer called your organization and told you they were seriously thinking of discontinuing five of your company's products, it would cause a chain reaction. Any business leader would look at a situation where potential significant financial loss would occur as requiring immediate attention — the jets would fire up and all hands would be on deck. Everyone would focus on that problem: analysts, futurists, sales people, financial advisors, supply chain employees, you name it — anyone in the business who could do something to fix the problem would be invited to the table. And no one would leave until a win/win solution was found to stop that customer from taking such extreme actions."

---

9 Jo Piazza, "Women of Color Hit a 'Concrete Ceiling' in Business," *Wall Street Journal* (New York, NY), September 27, 2016. (https://www.wsj.com/articles/women-of-color-hit-a-concrete-ceiling-in-business-1474963440).

"That's what an imperative looks like to me," I concluded.

And then I asked, "What if those leaders took the less urgent position of, 'Well, as long as we make *some* progress everyone should be happy, so we don't have to fix this issue today.' Would you be comfortable with that?"

Absolutely no one would accept that answer.

So why are we comfortable accepting the fact that women and people of color are underrepresented at mid-to-senior leadership and board levels? If it is an *imperative*, where is the team that is focusing on it? Truth be told, most line managers see diversity and inclusion as an "HR issue" or, better yet, a "diversity and inclusion officer's responsibility."

We must stop recognizing and rewarding people for simply making progress. It's too easy for organizations to receive awards and recognition for doing things that look good to the outside world but do little to actually move the needle. Rather, let's reward results. Let's reward equality.

There are many contributing factors as to why equality is not positioned as one of the top five imperatives on a CEO's agenda. But there's a new question that needs to be asked and answered: Why are we waiting for someone else to make the changes needed for women and people of color to advance? Why are we comfortable hearing that it will take 40 years for us to obtain parity? What about 100 years?

According to a recent study entitled *Women in the Workplace* conducted by McKinsey & Co. and LeanIn.org, it will take 100 years for women to catch up to the number of men in the C-suite.[10] Why are we not using our voices in bold and courageous ways to address this so-called *imperative*?

What is clear is that women aren't speaking loud enough. Women aren't doing what it takes to be heard, to be seen, to be viewed as a priority. We have deferred responsibility and ownership of the problem to men. We gather in our huddles and complain that "they" aren't doing anything about the problem. I can't deny that men are in the power seats to significantly impact the situation for the positive. They can certainly open doors for women and people of color.

But women have the power to open them too. So why don't we?

Are we afraid? Do we not know how to speak truth with power? Do we not understand each other? These are the kinds of questions I want to address in this book.

Years ago, when I was in the business world, I learned a leadership principle that shapes my thinking to this day. That principle is, "You are either a part of the problem or a part of the solution." Are we, as women, a part of the problem? Could it be that we need to embrace our own power and responsibilities in this area? Are we going to go down in history as being a part of limiting the advancement of other women and minorities?

---

10 LeanIn.org and McKinsey & Co., *Women in the Workplace Report 2016*, 2016. https://womenintheworkplace.com/.

We must have everyone doing their part to address this "unfinished business," as former Secretary of State Hillary Clinton called it. We have to speak to *more than just the companies* we work for. We need the *government to* get involved. We need *educators* to get involved. We need *parents* to get involved. The effort must start at the grade-school level with a focus on reshaping the perception of girls and children of other races along with the opportunities they have in life.

They say history is a great teacher. Perhaps it is time for women and people of color to look back and recognize that we are where we are today because other men and women were brave enough to say, "This is not right! And I am going to do something about it."

We are powerful, not powerless.
But we stir up conviction individually, and then we must find our collective voice.

Earlier this year, my conviction was stirred as never before.

I was sitting at a business development luncheon at Southern Methodist University in Dallas, Texas. The lunch was being held at the Bobby Lyle Engineering Building, and Bobby Lyle was sitting at the table where I was sitting. The mayor of Dallas was scheduled to address the audience but was running behind, and the emcee did a great job filling the void. He invited one of the guests also sitting at my table to come to the podium to say something about Bobby Lyle. The gentleman's name was Calvin

Stephens, a man whom I had met more than 10 years before. We had lost touch, and honestly, I really didn't know his story or very much about him.

Calvin began to tell a story about his life and the role Bobby Lyle played in his success. Calvin shared that he was one of the first African-American males to attend SMU back in the 1960s. He had graduated from a college in Houston and was encouraged to visit SMU, despite the fact that his family didn't have the finances or relationships to get him into such a prestigious university. Sure, he was smart, hardworking and could certainly succeed, but in his mind, he couldn't see how it would be possible.

As the story goes, at the insistence of his parents he made the trip to SMU and bumped into Bobby Lyle. They were both distracted as they were walking down the hall and literally, physically, bumped into each other. He and Bobby became instant friends.

Calvin secretly wondered to himself why this man was being so friendly to him. "What does he want from me?" he thought. But Bobby wanted nothing more than to help. In fact, Bobby Lyle wanted to do something that would change Calvin's life. He wanted to offer him a scholarship to attend SMU. Calvin accepted and eventually became one of the first African-American males to graduate from SMU.

As they got to know each other, Calvin asked Bobby about his passion to help others, particularly black students. Bobby, as you might have guessed by now, is a white male. Bobby told several moving stories to explain where his passion came from. And the one that impacted Calvin the most was this:

Bobby shared that in the '60s, there was a car wreck in Mississippi where he lived. Six children were in the car — five white children and one black. Six ambulances were deployed to the scene. Five ambulances came back with injured children, white children, but one came back empty. He couldn't understand why the black boy was left behind, why the black boy was left to die.

Bobby had several defining life experiences like this one. Each time, he would ask his mom why these injustices were not being addressed. Each time his mother would say, "It's not right, but it's the way that it is."

One day, the thought came to Bobby, *I must do something. I can't sit by any more and see things that I know are wrong and not do anything.* And so, his life's mission grew to help others — black, white, men and women of all backgrounds. He went on to achieve tremendous success in his life and used that success for the greater good.

It is truly a heartwarming story, but a very challenging one. How is it that we look around and see the inequities that women and minorities experience every day and not say a word? What will it take for us to become the drivers of change? What will it take for men and women to come together to stop injustices?

We can't keep showing up in the same old ways thinking that, magically, something new is going to happen. That's insanity. No, we have to muster the courage to say,

"It's not right, and I am going to do something about it. Starting today."

I hope this book will spark a burning desire in your heart to become a leader who goes down in history as doing something to correct the injustices in the business world. While there are so many injustices, this is one I know can be corrected. It starts with a simple conversation — as everything always does.

But we need *courageous conversations*. We need to talk about the things that no one wants to talk about. We need to have *real conversations*.

I hope the words, stories and insights contained in this book will inspire you to take action. Throughout the stories you read here, I pray you will be challenged to create your own stories. I pray for you and for me that one day others will say, "They had the courage to change the game."

It only takes one person to start a movement. Will you be that person?

One

Courageous Conversations About the Present Truth

"And the day came when the risk it took
to remain tight inside the bud was
more painful than the risk it took to
blossom."

—Anais Nin

It is without question that women and people of color
have made progress in many ways, yet the sad truth is
despite the fact that Hillary Clinton was the first female
presidential candidate of a major political party and
Barack Obama was the first black president, women and
people of color still struggle to achieve fair representation
in the business world and also struggle for fair compensation. The struggle is very real for women and people of
color in cultures where the dominant group looks, speaks
and behaves differently than the minority group, and the

minority group is expected to assimilate and behave as a member of the dominant group. The emotional stress of trying to behave in an inauthentic way can be overwhelming, resulting in disengagement and turnover. The call of this book is for women to stop waiting for men to solve the inequalities that hinder the success of women and people of color. It is time for men and women of all backgrounds and ethnicities to step up, come together to form a louder voice, and launch a sincere, authentic and real movement to achieve equality.

A CHANGED REALITY

In January 2015, I had the honor of participating in the inaugural *Women Who Spark* recognition luncheon, and the White House Director of Technology, Megan Smith, delivered the keynote address.

Megan began her keynote address by asking a couple of questions. She first asked how many knew of the contributions of a lady by the name of Margaret Hamilton. A few folks in the room raised their hands. I had no clue.

She then asked who knew of the contributions of a woman by the name of Katherine Johnson. More people in the audience raised their hands. Again, I was at a loss. She comforted the audience by saying we shouldn't be disappointed if we didn't know who these women were. Education, history and entertainment have never captured the true contributions of these women.

She went on to share a little bit about their accomplishments.

It was Margaret Hamilton who took Apollo 11 to the moon. She was the engineer, mathematician and software scientist who made it possible for Neil Armstrong and Buzz Aldrin to walk on the moon. The lunar landing was one of the first times that software was ever entrusted with such a mission-critical, real-time task. And the application development work for that feat was placed in the hands of Margaret Hamilton. Hamilton taught herself to program and had risen to become director of the Software Engineering Division of the MIT Instrumentation Laboratory, which developed the computer under contract to NASA.[11]

And Katherine Johnson? She is an American physicist, space scientist and mathematician who contributed to America's aeronautics and space programs with the early application of digital electronic computers at NASA. Known for accuracy in computerized celestial navigation, she calculated the trajectory for Project Mercury and the 1969 Apollo 11 flight to the moon. Dissatisfied with teaching, Johnson decided on a career in mathematics. At a family gathering, a relative mentioned that the National Advisory Committee for Aeronautics (NACA), later to become NASA, was looking for new people. They especially wanted African-American women for their Guidance and Navigation Department. Johnson was offered a job

11 Karen Tegan Padir, "Software – and a Woman – at the Heart of Lunar Triumph," *Wired*, https://www.wired.com/insights/2014/08/software-woman-heart-lunar-triumph/.

in 1953, and she immediately accepted.[12] The rest, as they say, is history — only this history hasn't been sufficiently told or celebrated.

These women were pioneers and innovators. They were self-taught. They did things that had never been done before, and they impacted the world in profound ways. Perhaps you, like me, knew nothing about these women or their contributions.

Just for giggles, I asked 10 of my colleagues and friends if they were familiar with the work of these women. They were all like me — clueless. One could argue that because my background is not in technology, it wouldn't be surprising that I'd never heard of these women. I would have to disagree. For more than a decade, I have been studying women, minorities and inequalities in the workplace. I have published books, written blogs and given speeches highlighting the contributions of these people. And as a black female, I have been particularly interested in learning more about the contributions of women from my ethnicity.

As I continued to listen to Megan that day, I was blinded by a light of the obvious: Women *still* aren't recognized for their contributions, despite the fact that we have been a major part of shaping history!

It made me think about the many opportunities that women and people of varying ethnic backgrounds are not being afforded. The data is so loud and clear as to the

---

12 Wikipedia contributors, "Katherine Johnson," *Wikipedia, The Free Encyclopedia,* https://en.wikipedia.org/w/index.php?title=Katherine_Johnson&oldid=778521976.

benefits of having women and minorities in senior leadership and board positions. Yet despite these facts, *there has been only slow progress even though these groups are more pronounced in the workforce than ever before.*

I will refer throughout the book to this dynamic of continued inequality as a "changed reality." And I am appealing to all who read this book to ask themselves a question:

Are you *responding* to — or *reacting* to — this changed reality?

Consider these facts that point to a changed reality:

- According to the U.S. Department of Commerce's Minority Business Development Agency's report *Minority Population Growth: 1995 to 2050*, over the next 40 years, 85 percent of U.S. population growth will come from non-white ethnic groups.
- While purchasing dollars among whites increased 139 percent between 1990–2008, growth was 337 percent among Asians, 213 percent among Native Americans and 187 percent among African Americans during the same time period. The difference is even more dramatic among Hispanics, whose buying power rocketed 349 percent compared to growth of only 141 percent among non-Hispanics during the same period.[13]

---

13 Jeffrey Matthew Humphreys, *The Multicultural Economy 2008*. Athens, GA: Selig Center for Economic Growth, Terry College of Business, University of Georgia, 2008.

- Women are 47 percent of the workforce and growing.[14] In fact, 70 percent of all new entries into the workforce over the next five years will be immigrants, women and people of color.[15]
- If we were at parity regarding the CEOs of Fortune 500 companies, there would be 233 female, 73 African American and 63 Latino CEOs.
  - The Fortune 500 CEO reality today? Four African Americans, nine Asians, six Latinos, 18 women and the rest are white men.[16]
  - Not only are the CEO positions primarily held by the dominant group, but so are the board seats in America. In 2004, white men held 71.2 percent of board seats associated with the nation's Fortune 100 companies. By 2010 that figure had decreased slightly to 69.9 percent. During that same period, women gained 16 board seats — with five occupied

---

14 Crosby Burns, Kimberly Barton, and Sophia Kerby, *The State of Diversity in Today's Workforce Report*, The Center for American Progress, July 12, 2012. https://www.americanprogress.org/issues/economy/reports/2012/07/12/11938/the-state-of-diversity-in-todays-workforce/.

15 Diana Stork, Fiona Wilson, Andrea Wicks Bowles, "The New Workforce Reality: Insights for Today, Implications for Tomorrow," *Simmons School of Management and Bright Horizons Family Solutions*, 2005.

16 Alliance for Board Diversity, *Missing Pieces: Women and Minorities on Fortune 500 Boards—2010 Alliance for Board Diversity Census, 2011*, Revised July 21, 2011. http://theabd.org/abd_report.pdf.

by minority women. But that growth represented a mere 1.1 percent increase for women on corporate boards over six years.[17]

With the release of the movie *Hidden Figures*, many people realized there was a huge piece of history left out of textbooks we should have learned about...from women of color. Now we are finally learning about this piece of history. And it's about damn time.

THE FIVE BRUTAL FACTS FOR OBTAINING EQUALITY

The world-famous book by Jim Collins, *Good to Great*, offers several principles that contribute to a company experiencing greatness. One of the principles includes confronting the brutal facts.

There are five brutal facts that must be considered if we are truly to obtain equality:

Brutal Fact #1: The vast majority of companies are still operating off of old paradigms, and their leaders don't know how to manage the most diverse workforce in history.

Brutal Fact #2: Women and minorities are making extremely slow progress in advancement in the business world.

---

17 Ibid.

Brutal Fact #3: Most of the research that has been done to understand the plight of women has focused on white women. Little insight has been afforded to the world about the experience of the non-white female in the business world.

Brutal Fact #4: Women have unintentionally become part of the problem.

Brutal Fact #5: Organizations haven't established nor held leaders accountable for demonstrating inclusive behaviors.

Here's a change statistic for you: More than half of the companies that were industry leaders in 1955 were still industry leaders in 1990. But more than two-thirds of the 1990 industry leaders no longer existed by 2004.[18]

What is behind this dynamic? There are many contributing factors, but at the end of the day from my perspective the numerous contributing factors can be summed up in one word — leadership. Companies like Blockbuster, Circuit City, Kodak and the many others refused to acknowledge and deal with change.

Many of these companies fell off the grid because they failed to innovate. They failed to recognize that the consumer's desires were shifting and they failed to diagnose the needs and complexities of a changed workforce. Their

18 Dane Stangler and Sam Arbesman, "What Does Fortune 500 Turnover Mean?" *Ewing Marion Kauffman Foundation*, 2012. http://www.kauffman.org/~/media/kauffman_org/research%20reports%20and%20covers/2012/06/fortune_500_turnover.pdf.

organizations became dysfunctional, slow and unable to collaborate. They failed to increase speed to bring new products to market and were unable to execute new strategies to remain relevant, including new talent management strategies.

I believe the warning signs are clear about the continued changes that will occur for the workforce as more women graduate from college than men and as a higher percentage of multicultural employees enter the workforce. America is browning. Truth be told, America was brown before it was ever white. The data also suggests that only business leaders who embrace the change, who recognize the changing face of the consumer and make the needed cultural change that allows everyone to engage in an authentic way at work will survive. Future successful leaders will have to embrace female leaders and drive equality if they want to innovate to meet the needs of the changing consumer. And although many organizations tout diversity and inclusion as a business imperative, few are taking any meaningful steps to drive equality. As Dr. Mitchell Hammer puts it, "Your success in achieving workplace goals is better served when you are able to more deeply understand culturally learned differences, recognize commonalities between yourself and others, and act on this increased insight in culturally appropriate ways that facilitate performance, learning and personal growth among diverse groups."[19]

---

19 Mitchell R. Hammer in conjunction with Intercultural Development Inventory, LLC, "Organization – Sample Individual Profile Report,"

Everyone has heard the old adage "You snooze, you lose." But in today's marketplace where change is constant and ever-increasing, if leaders of an organization fail to keep their eye on the ball or get lulled into believing that success is a given, the loss could be — and HAS BEEN — the company itself.

The truth is that *everything has changed*: The workforce. The way we work. The way we communicate. The consumer. Technology. The economy. The list goes on and on.

In the old world of "life as we know it," change was controllable. The workforce wasn't as diverse. Consumers weren't driving the market. Upper-level management was in control. And it felt good.

Now things are different. Becoming a leader who can properly manage all of this requires us to make a mental shift. It requires that we challenge our worldview, particularly as it relates to women and people of color.

ANTICIPATING CHANGE & ADDRESSING BIAS: THE TEA LEAVES SPEAK

There are and will be many dynamic leaders who will obtain success for their organizations by implementing effective initiatives and utilizing the latest technology. However, without a concerted and meaningful talent management change initiative that focuses on equality,

---

Intercultural Development v. 3(IDI), 2012. https://idiinventory.com/wp-content/themes/evolution/pdfs/Jose_-_Exemplar_-_Profile_-_August_2012.pdf.

companies will fail to get the most from their employees. Successful leaders are gaining new appreciation for the need to build cultural competencies. They are becoming more sensitive to the negative impact of bias, racism and even privilege. Recently, in one of my transformational leadership programs a black female engaged in a spirited conversation with a white male about the realities of having a black son. She said to the man, "I had to have the 'talk' when he was really little." The white male had no idea what the "talk" was. The talk is about what to do (not if, but when) you are pulled over by a police officer. Some people refer to the high percentage of black men that get pulled over "driving while black." Her white male counterpart was astonished. He couldn't believe that this was a reality. It stirred an emotion within him. When we become more aware and engage in courageous conversations we start to get a different appreciation for all that people are dealing with. He asked this lady how this impacts her on a daily basis and she shared that some days she is really nervous. It hit him that she brings this to work every day and he became extremely empathic towards her. He even asked her if she would be willing to let him know when she is dealing with the emotions so that he could become a better leader and not make assumptions about what was on her mind or wonder why she might be a little somber on a particular day.

I have observed senior leadership falling into three categories as it relates to change in the business world:

Leadership Group #1: The Ostriches
They stick their head in the ground and refuse to change.
Leadership Group #2: The Deny-ers
They deny change is happening and insist that what-ever is happening in the universe won't have any meaningful impact on their watch.
Leadership Group #3: The Curve Jumpers
They *intentionally* do what is referred to as jumping the curve. The theory behind jumping the curve is simple: What goes up must come down… unless a new curve is created.

Paul Nunes and Tim Breene, the authors of the book *Jumping the S-Curve: How to Beat the Growth Cycle, Get on Top, and Stay There*, offer great insight on what high-performing teams and organizations do to continuously reinvent themselves. The concept of jumping the curve is not new. In fact, it goes back to the 1800s when America was growing by leaps and bounds.

Sometimes it is wise to read the tea leaves, take old models and apply them to new situations. And it is ALWAYS wise to make change work for you and build your change agility muscle.

So why such slow progress overall?

There has been much debate about the contributing factors to the slow progress for women and minorities. Thought leaders have suggested that it is organizational culture. Others have prompted the idea that women need to do more. Even others have suggested that it is policy-related. The research conducted for this book suggests that the major contributing factor can be summed up in one word. One word that explains everything.

And that word is BIAS.

We all have biases. Biases can be conscious or unconscious. Conscious bias shows up as racism, but most of what happens in the business world is related to unconscious bias.

Unconscious biases are prevalent in all of us, shaping our worldview and expectations of others. The disconcerting fact is that those unconscious biases can be contrary to our conscious beliefs. America and corporate America will never reach their greatest levels of success unless we find the courage to acknowledge, own and take action to address unconscious biases. Why? These biases cause us to have a certain worldview about others who are different than ourselves. Unconscious biases make us think the way we think is best — the right way, the only way.

Where do these unconscious biases come from? How do we even identify them? And once we do identify them, why and how do we change them?

First things first: According to *Implicit Bias* by Jerry Kang, UCLA School of Law professor, a few of our common unconscious biases come from our direct experiences with other people, events, situations, etc. However, the majority of our biases, both positive and negative, are based on vicarious experiences — those relayed to us through other people, stories, books, movies, media and culture. Kang continues by sharing:

> One way to find out about bias is simply to ask people. However, in a post-civil rights environment, it has become much less useful to ask explicit questions on sensitive topics. We run into a "willing and able" problem. Many people simply are not willing to tell researchers — or anyone — what they really feel. They may be chilled by an air of political correctness.[20]

Second, and more important, when it comes to bias people may not even *know* what is inside their heads. Indeed, a wealth of cognitive psychology has demonstrated that we are lousy at introspection. For example, even slight environmental changes alter our judgments and behavior without our realization. If the room smells of Lysol, people eat more neatly. People holding a warm cup of coffee versus a cold cup ascribe warmer personality traits to a stranger described in a vignette. We are easily and subconsciously swayed to alter our thoughts and opinions based on sometimes uncontrollable influences.

In the workplace, managers are frequently guilty of allowing bias to negatively infiltrate and impact employee

---

20 Jerry Kang, "Implicit Bias: A Primer for Courts," August 2009. http://jerrykang.net/research/2009-implicit-bias-primer-for-courts/.

engagement, collaboration and even advancement for women and people of color. Most of what you see in corporate America is not blatant racism (although that does occur), but it is rather what researchers refer to as unconscious bias.

Consider this example: A group of employees composed of line managers, human resource representatives and diversity and inclusion professionals are sitting around a table discussing future talent. This usually happens once a year in every organization. There is a list of employees who are considered as "ready now," there are others who are deemed as "high potential but ready in two years," and there are usually two other categories: "solid contributor but no upward potential" and "contributor and a blocker," which refers to someone who is in a certain job function but the individual has no aspirations of doing anything else.

If an employee is not anywhere on this list, then they are probably already on a performance improvement plan and are on their way out the door.

During this conversation, one of the line managers recommends that Paula, a black female, is ready for promotion. As each of the other managers reviews Paula, one of the line manager's colleagues says, "She just isn't leadership material." No one challenges the thinking process of this decision-maker who is clearly not comfortable with Paula, although he offers no explanation.

For this decision-maker, "She just isn't leadership material" is code for "I am not comfortable with this person's potential management style. Her style doesn't reflect what I believe. It doesn't reflect *my* style, and therefore, it cannot be good." Despite Paula being ready, capable and an excellent contributor, she gets passed over for a promotion opportunity. This is unconscious bias at its best.

I will go into more detail about what can be done about addressing unconscious bias in subsequent chapters. What you should know for now is that this is a common example and explains why more women and minorities are not being afforded opportunities. They have to *make* others become comfortable with them, and women of varying ethnicities have to work even harder.

IDENTIFYING AND OVERCOMING UNCONSCIOUS BIASES

Still not sure exactly what unconscious biases are? Or maybe you think you don't have any? I'm talking about the following types of unconscious beliefs and stereotypes that infiltrate our society and, therefore, corporate America. For instance:

- Men are better leaders.
- White men are smarter.
- African-American men are good athletes.
- African-American women are "angry."
- White women are great trophy wives.
- All women are on the "mommy track."
- Latino men are lazy.
- Latino women are extremely emotional.
- Asian men are good at technology.

- Asian women are quiet.
- Native-American men are drunks.
- Native-American women are submissive.

In 1995, doctors Anthony Greenwald and Mahzarin R. Banaji theorized that it was possible that our social behavior was not completely under our conscious control. Advances in neuroscience and other social sciences have helped us understand that people can consciously believe in equality while simultaneously acting on subconscious prejudices they are not aware of.[21]

Three years after this theory was developed, Dr. Greenwald designed a bias test. The test is referred to as the Implicit Association Test (IAT). This assessment has been widely used in the field of neuropsychology and helps people understand the dynamics of their personal attributes, including identification of conscious and unconscious biases.

I challenge you to take the IAT at https://implicit.harvard.edu/implicit/.[22] Why? So you can start touching your truth. Enough of the political correctness — let's tell the truth for a change.

---

21 John A. Powell, "Reading Between the Lines: Uncovering Unconscious Bias" (presentation at the Unconscious Bias Panel sponsored by the Writers Guild of America West, Screen Actors Guild, Americans for American Values and the Kirwan Institute, Los Angeles, CA, September 30, 2009).

22 Tony Greenwald, Mahzarin Banaji, Brian Nosek, Bethany Teachman, and Matt Nock, "Project Implicit," Harvard University, 2011. https://implicit.harvard.edu/implicit/.

And the truth is that each of us holds biases, and these biases impact the way we see people who are different from us.

Once we are each consciously aware and can honestly identify and engage in courageous conversations about our negative unconscious biases, we can then learn ways to talk through, overcome and change them. We will all benefit from doing this, our careers will benefit, those around us will benefit, our organizations will benefit, our future generations will benefit, and yes, as glib as it sounds, the world will benefit.

ESCAPING OUR COMFORT ZONE AND CHALLENGING OUR MINDSET

It is time. Time to draw a line in the sand and discover what we *truly* believe, then challenge those beliefs to promote inclusion. And it starts with you and me.

Change like this requires learning. It requires pushing outside of that comfort zone. It was John F. Kennedy who said, "Leadership and learning are indispensable to each other." I couldn't agree more. Unfortunately, there are not a lot of leaders who believe in the power of learning. They have risen to the ranks of the C-suite and stopped growing. As if rising to the higher ranks automatically equipped them with everything they would ever need to know to remain successful and relevant.

But it's just not true. It is time to escape the comfort zone, once and for all. As T. Harv Eker said, "Nobody ever died of discomfort, yet living in the name of comfort has killed more ideas, more opportunities, more actions, and more growth than everything else combined. Comfort kills!"

Learning requires that we adopt a growth mindset. We have to believe that we are capable of learning. If we are to close the representation gap for women, both men and women must believe that is it attainable.

We must embrace a *mindset* of possibility thinking. Let me explain in a bit more detail. *Mindset* is a simple idea discovered by world-renowned Stanford University psychologist Carol Dweck (Ph.D.) after decades of research on achievement and success — it is a simple idea that makes all the difference.

In a *fixed* mindset, people believe their basic qualities like intelligence or talent are simply fixed traits. They spend their time documenting their intelligence or talent instead of developing it. They also believe that talent alone creates success — without effort.

In a *growth* mindset, people believe that their most basic abilities can be developed through dedication and hard work — brains and talent are just the starting point. This view creates a love of learning and a resilience that is essential for great accomplishment. Virtually all great people have had these qualities. They understand that no one has ever accomplished great things — not Mozart, Darwin or Michael Jordan — without years of passionate practice and learning.

It is going to take each of us raising our awareness and taking ownership for how we think about taking on the challenge of women, men, race and equality in the business world. We are going to have to get curious and practice.

Dweck argues that each of us is constantly engaged in an internal conversation about whether or not we can experience success.

She suggests four steps to help us move into the growth mindset: [23]

1. **Learn to listen to your fixed mindset.**

   You can't change what you don't acknowledge. When you think about equality in the workplace, is your first thought that it is a challenge way too big to take on? Or do you automatically think you're not equipped to take on this challenge? Both of these thoughts represent a fixed mindset and will stop you from embracing what I will share with you during the rest of the book.

2. **Recognize that you have a choice.**

   Dweck explains, "How you interpret challenges, setbacks and criticism is your choice. You can interpret them in a fixed mindset as signs that your fixed talents or abilities are lacking. Or you can interpret them in a growth mindset as signs that you need to ramp up your strategies and effort,

---

23 Carol Dweck, *Mindset: The New Psychology of Success* (New York: Ballentine Books, 2006).

stretch yourself and expand your abilities. It's up to you."

Every one of us has experienced times where we had to slow down and recognize the power of our choice. Every one of us knows the impact of making good and bad choices. I am asking that you make an intentional choice to be a leader who is dedicated to driving equality.

3. **Talk back to the fixed mindset voice with a growth mindset voice.**

So much of what helps us achieve success is our ability to convince ourselves that we can do what we have set as a goal or an aspiration. In the book penned by Siimon Reynolds, *Why People Fail: The 16 Obstacles to Success and How You Can Overcome Them*, Reynolds features the practice of a number of athletes including Derek Jeter. Jeter shared that he would talk to himself about performing well enough to be recognized as the MVP. Jeter's practice of talking to himself occurred on a daily basis, sometimes as many as 200 times per day.

Practice saying to yourself, "We can do this. We can achieve equality, and I will play a role."

4. **Take the growth mindset action.**

We all have heard it said that knowledge is power. I don't agree. I believe that knowledge becomes powerful when action is taken.

Throughout the course of this book, I will be challenging you to think about your beliefs, values, habits, behaviors and patterns as they relate to driving equality. Checking ourselves in these critical areas is what will lead to the breakthrough.

If you agree with even half of what you have read in this first chapter, I hope that something has been stirred inside of you. I hope that your conscience has been touched and you are open to helping create a future where not only you will experience equality, but your children and their children will too.

COURAGEOUS CALL-TO-ACTION REFLECTION QUESTIONS

- What changes have you noticed in the workplace, workforce and in consumers?
- Do you acknowledge that it is time to develop new leadership behaviors to engage in a world with a changed reality? What happens if we don't make these changes?
- Do you believe in the power of equality? Why?
- How have you demonstrated inclusive behaviors as a leader, and how have you shown yourself to be a public champion for great talent across differences?
- Are you willing to closely examine your values, habits, behaviors and patterns to step out and speak out as an authentic believer in equality? How will you assess your own beliefs?

Two

Courageous Conversations About the Role of Women

"There is a special place in hell for
women who do not help other women."

—Madeleine Albright

I have heard it said and have said myself that *great leaders live in truth.*

Okay, so here's the truth: Unintentionally, women have become part of the reason why diversity and inclusion have not advanced in the business world. Shocking, right? You can close your mouth now if you like.

The sad reality is that women have been so busy blaming others (mostly white men) that we have taken our eyes off *our own* truth. Our truth is that we own a big piece of the picture. We have biases against each other. And most of these biases, as for everyone, have been shaped by society and by the media.

It's time for all of us to examine the biases that are holding women back from boldly serving as champions for other women. This is not only important in our professional life but in our personal life as well. It's time that we talk about the reality.

WHY AREN'T WOMEN ANSWERING THE CALL?

Kellie A. McElhaney, Ph.D., is a professor at UC Berkeley. She shared with me two enlightening experiences that revealed why many women may not see the importance of connecting with one another and may be shying away from courageous conversations. Kelly shared with me that she was in Dubai delivering a leadership development session for 20 women. She told me she asked the group of women what female leader they admired from around the world. She said it was interesting was that not one woman in the group could identify a single woman whom they held in high regard. These were women from around the world and the middle to senior leadership levels. They worked for global organizations.

"I was shocked," shared Kellie. "These were young, smart, female leaders and not one of them could relate to another woman in leadership. It caused me to ask myself several questions: Were women not connecting because of generational differences? Was it because of ethnic background? Was it because of stage of life? Were women not aware of the great achievements of other women who had broken through? I just couldn't understand.[24]

That's both the problem and the opportunity.

Conversations simply aren't being had among women. We don't understand each other, and there's never really been a call for us to intentionally connect.

The call requires women to invest in other women across differences. The call is for *all* women to become inspiring public advocates and champions for other women. The research I conducted to write this book proves that we don't know each other. Women we interviewed didn't comprehend or weren't aware that that the research up until the last few years has been primarily about white women.

Women haven't acknowledged that we have biases against each other, and those biases impact how we treat each other. And we don't know that our journeys in corporate America are different. Some multicultural women or women of color doubt that white women even care about them or their success. If white women don't really care about each other, then this isn't a surprise.

At the 2016 AOL Makers Conference, Sheryl Sandberg expanded her own view of the problem when she indicated that women are a long way from achieving equality

---

24 Kellie A. McElhaney, Ph.D., in a discussion with the author, December 2015.

due to the biases of both men and women. Finally, a leader of her caliber tells the truth! She also boldly stated that while companies profess their commitment to diversity, employees aren't buying in. The younger generations of leaders don't understand why it is still a work in progress; they thought more progress had been made.

Dianne Wyatt, a white female senior executive with Frito-Lay, shared her perspective: "Ten years ago, I would have said there was no difference between the experiences that white women were having as compared to women of color. I would have said that all women were having the same experience. But then there was a pivotal point in my career. I was working with the SVP of Finance over an issue, and we had a transparent and thoughtful conversation. I was able to solve that problem because he trusted me and knew me. I was able to drive my business results because I had been in corporate and had driven my career for 20 years. He knew my track record and respected me because of what I had accomplished.

"I was privileged over women of color because there weren't any women of color when I started. I had those connections that they didn't. We have to minimize risk. So, white men or white women aren't going to extend trust and neither will women of color. The challenge you have right now is that a lot of people do believe that everyone else's journey is like our own — that's too self-centered. But when I fully owned and understood mine was different, THAT was when I understood that I was able to drive results that a woman of color wouldn't have been able to because of connections.

"My realization was this: Women of color have to work twice as hard and prove themselves sometimes two or three times more than a white female. I didn't realize that before."[25]

As you read this chapter, what's your story? Do you think all women in corporate America are having the same experience? Are you aware, if you are a white female, of your privilege?

So how do we get more white women to gain an appreciation for our differences?

We have to engage in courageous conversations. We have to be honest with each other. And, most important, we have to share our stories, sensitizing each other in a deep emotional way.

I made a strategic mistake in this area myself.

My daughter, MaryEllen, is now 29 years old. As she was growing up, I so wanted to convince her that the world would eagerly await her. I had the conversation about the challenges that women face. I even had the conversation about the unique challenges that women of color face in building a successful career. But what I didn't do was prepare her for the fact that other women were not going to necessarily be her first line of support. Let me explain.

I wanted MaryEllen, as most parents do, to follow in my footsteps and pursue a career in corporate America.

---

25 Dianne Wyatt in a discussion with the author, May 2, 2015.

After she graduated from Louisiana State University with a degree in communications, I convinced her to try corporate America. She was reluctant but wanted to make good money, so she took a job at a local company in Dallas where her childhood friend also worked.

"This is going to be great," she shared with me. "I just hope that people will accept me." I asked her what she meant. "I am going to work for a baby boomer, Mom. I hope that she will respect me." I convinced her that she would.

Boy, was I wrong. Just a few months into her new job, her white female baby-boomer manager wrote her up. What for, you ask? For asking too many questions and challenging the status quo. I know, right?!

I have to admit, I had an immediate emotional reaction. She came home one day with a document indicating she had been "insubordinate." I could hardly console MaryEllen — she had always been a high achiever.

What was going wrong? Her manager didn't want to be questioned or challenged. She didn't want any new ideas despite the company's commitment to innovation. I became the helicopter mom from hell. I took the document that her manager had presented and tore it apart, writing what turned out to be a seven-page document about the company's onboarding process, their commitment to diversity and, finally, their commitment to helping their leaders build the capability to manage multiple generations.

Long story short, a few months later, the manager was let go. Sadly, my daughter resigned, confused and emotionally exhausted. The good news is that she found her calling as a teacher. She has a great job shaping the lives of little first graders at a private school just outside of Dallas.

Are women really willing to support other women? I don't know.

Let me ask you a question: What woman or women are you pouring into? Who are you creating new advancement opportunities for? How are you challenging the status quo, particularly in succession planning, to ensure an equal slate? Or are you silent?

Just stop for a minute and think about how you are showing up for other women.

WOMEN SUPPORTING WOMEN [WHAT WOMEN MUST GET BETTER AT DOING]

History provides such powerful lessons if we will simply pause to study it.

In the mid-1950s, Ella Fitzgerald was a rising vocal artist. Her sultry sound was new and fresh. There was just one big problem: Ella could not get booked at many of the hottest nightclubs because she was a black artist. She really wanted to be featured at the Mocambo, *the* Hollywood nightclub where careers were made.

Marilyn Monroe was a star at the time and was getting calls to perform at all of the nightclubs. She heard about the challenges Ella was facing and decided to take action. She and Ella had become friends, so Marilyn leveraged her power. She called the club's manager and promised that if they would feature Ella, she would commit to come to her performances and sit in the front row every night for a week, knowing her presence would motivate the press to cover Ella's performances. Her strategy worked.

On March 15, 1955, Ella played a show that put her career on a path to stardom, dubbing her the "Queen of Jazz" and going on to record more than 70 albums, forever changing the music industry.

Ella and Marilyn created their own sisterhood — such a moving story of a woman publicly supporting another woman.

Marilyn clearly recognized that she had the power, and she made the choice to use it. She didn't worry about the perception that might be formulated about her supporting a black woman. She didn't care that some might say that she was "carrying the equality" banner. No, instead she did what *all* women should do for each other. She had a seat at the table of opportunity, and she pulled up a chair so that Ella could also take a seat.

Let me again pose the question to you: What women are *you* investing in? I am not talking about the woman to whom you said, "Call me and we'll do lunch." I am not even talking about mentoring, though mentoring does serve a role of its own. I am talking about sponsorship, about boldly, publicly, shamelessly and intentionally opening the door of opportunity for another woman.

And why not take it one step further, doing it for a woman who is not from your race or generation?

What's interesting is that men have been doing this for years, particularly if they are from the same demographic, and *especially* if they're members of the dominant group.

Men have no problem promoting or sponsoring other men, and they make no apology for it. It is all under the premise that they are promoting someone who is good, which begs the question, do we as women not see other women as being great leaders? Has society shaped our image of what a great leader looks like so that we, too, default to the characteristics of white men?

Black men do this to a lesser degree. They, too, struggle with the potential of a label being placed on them if they promote other black men. It is said that the first step in growth is admitting the truth about your starting point.

There is another truth that gives me hope. If we all slow down and think about who has helped us in our careers, perhaps you, like me, will recall that for the vast majority of the time It has been white men who have opened doors and made connections. So, some white men are already committed and have been committed to equality. The problem is that we don't have enough to make a significant impact. Well, the truth about women supporting women is not so good.

What does this mean? How could this be the case? I know for me personally that it has been white men who have opened doors for me — not white women. And to a very limited degree, it has also been multicultural men and/or women.

In 2001, shortly after founding The Center for Workforce Excellence, I conducted a series of informational interviews. I was trying to cut my learning curve and look to other women who I thought would be willing to share their experiences.

I interviewed two white women and one black woman who were all corporate consultants and trainers. I had this crazy idea that women would be willing to share what they had learned about being entrepreneurs. What happened next blew me away.

The two white women told me I would have success if I focused on helping black people but to not try to offer my services to white men or women. The black woman told me the questions I was asking made her uncomfortable, and she didn't want to share her proprietary information.

Take that for women supporting women! The good news is that fueled a commitment in me then to help every female entrepreneur I could. I hope history will show that I did just that. What will history reveal about *your* choices to support and help other women?

Victoria Felker shares her perspective on this: "Women are afraid to be seen as carrying the 'women banner.' As a result, we shy away from promoting other women. I was given some bad advice as I started to climb the ladder — to not be seen as too aggressive on supporting women's initiatives, and simply be known for driving great business results. What I have discovered is that I *can* do both and *need* to do both."[26]

---

26 Victoria Felker in a discussion with the author, December 14, 2015.

We need to turn to each other, not against each other. We have more in common than we know.

LOOKING THROUGH THE LENS OF OUR OWN ETHNO-BUBBLES

In the 2001 publication *Our Separate Ways*, one of the first books to compare and contrast the backgrounds and career paths of successful black and white women in corporate America, Dr. Ella Bell noted that many of the biases and stereotypes we hold — that race, poverty, a lack of education, dysfunctional family life or sexual prejudice are impediments to professional success — are not always true. These findings were based on her groundbreaking multiyear study into the life journeys of black and white female managers and executives.

While women share many commonalities, most white women don't realize or even begin to understand the aforementioned stereotypes that women of color must face and overcome on a daily basis in corporate America and in the world.

"There are some women who are advancing, but I'm not sure they're advancing evenly," said Regenia Stein, a black executive at Kraft. "Women of color still have a harder road."[27]

Stein was one of 18 professional women interviewed between December 2011 and March 2012 about the interactions and support between varying ethnic groups

27 Regenia Stein in a discussion with the author, January 11, 2012.

of women in the workplace. The interviewees included women who were black, white, bi-racial, Latina and Asian, all spread across a variety of occupations. Most of the women were corporate executives, but there were others who were researchers, judges and college professors.

Though their experiences and views ranged, they did agree on several notions. The foremost being that even in the midst of still-prevalent gender bias, white women have made significant strides. Further, most of the women of color spoke to there being some level of tension between their group and white women. And, finally, many of the women believed they understood the kinds of experiences white women were having in the workplace, but they recognized that they have little direct knowledge of what women of color experience.

"These are topics that speak to the doubts many women have about each other and that help to build the plastic walls that stop women from helping other women in organizational America," said Dr. Ancella Livers of the Center for Creative Leadership. "We see each other, but *don't* touch and often *can't* touch because the walls of our mistrust often impede communication beyond a shallow level."[28]

But these walls are not the only issues that are keeping women apart. It's as if women are floating in their own ethno-bubbles which distort their view of women from

---

28 Ancella Livers in an interview with Jenny Claggett, February 29, 2012.

other racial and ethnic groups and keep them from even trying to understand the varied experiences they all have.

While the plastic walls keep women from helping each other,
the ethno-bubbles keep them from identifying with each other or,
in many cases, from even trying to identify.

There are, of course, clear examples in which white women *have* helped women of color reach senior roles. Perhaps the most spectacular of these was in 2009 when Anne Mulcahy, a white woman and former CEO of Xerox, passed the mantle of her position to Ursula Burns, who is the current CEO of Xerox and the first African-American woman to hold the CEO position in a Fortune 500 company.

Yet in spite of such a high-profile example of support and recognition of talent across racial lines, or perhaps *because of* it, many other women are looking at their circumstances and wondering who will advocate for them.

"I would describe the relationship between women of color and white women in corporate America as *an uneasy truce,*" said Dr. Stacey Blake-Beard, a black female professor at Simmons College.[29]

Kelly Hannum, a white woman from the Center for Creative Leadership, agreed. "I do think women of color

---

29 Stacey Blake-Beard in a discussion with the author, February 14, 2012.

are doubly disadvantaged. How those disadvantages show up, I don't really know. I know what the research is, but I don't have the [personal] experience [of living with these disadvantages]."[30]

According to *The White House Project: Benchmarking Women's Leadership*, although women of color seem to be in management or administrative roles at the same percentage in which they are in the labor force, 11.5 percent and 11.8 percent respectively, they are not making it into the senior ranks of organizations. The problem seems to be based on issues other than competency. The White House report stated:

Studies show that African-American women's leadership tends to be impeded by negative, race-based stereotypes, frequent questioning of credibility and authority, and a lack of institutional support. Asian women report the lack of key professional relationships as a major obstacle, and Latina women frequently comment that corporate policies impede close relationships with extended family, which is a key source of support for their professional success.[31]

---

30 Kelly Hannum in a discussion with the author, February 14, 2012.

31 The White House Project, *The White House Project: Benchmarking Women's Leadership*, 2009, https://www.in.gov/icw/files/benchmark_wom_leadership.pdf.

This is where the plastic walls really begin to rise.

Though women seem to agree that on some level they need to support each other, even if it is only through sharing information, their ability to do so often seems impeded because of their disparate experience and perspectives. It is in this kind of support — information sharing, mentorship and sponsorship, for example — where race and gender often part paths.

Even so, a number of women of color we interviewed, regardless of their race or ethnicity, spoke of the strong and effective relationships they had with white women. In fact, these personal bonds have helped women of color navigate organizational ranks.

"But unless you forge a personal bond, the relationships are like those of young children," said Valerie Lewis, a black female attorney and senior executive for Safeway. "You know, they say boys play *near* each other; they don't play *with* each other."[32]

Herein lies the issue within the issue — it can be difficult to create those individual interactions if both parties are not receptive to building relationships. And many women of color believe their exchanges with white women are fraught with unacknowledged tensions and judgments.

Karen Kim (not her real name), an Asian-American management consultant who asked to remain anonymous, said she understands the stress between white women

---

32 Valerie Lewis in a discussion with the author, July 17, 2014.

and people of color from her own experience. "The tensions are not recognized or talked about," she said. "If you bring it up, and I have, carefully, I think white women are either going to deny it or gloss it over."[33]

The belief of many, particularly women of color, is that white women recognize their own gender but do not acknowledge how their race — their whiteness — influences their perspective of others. White women seem to categorize women of color and make decisions based on the view through their own ethno-bubble. But they aren't alone. The ethno-bubbles also frame how women of color understand their own experience and help create a negative resonance based on previous racial experiences. In essence, the ethno-bubbles of race shape women's understanding of the situation and help build the plastic walls that keep women from sharing and learning from their different perspectives.

Nowhere is this effect more evident than in the relationships between black and white women. While it is true that many black and white women have had deep and productive work and personal relationships, it is also clear that the most pervasive workplace tensions are between these two groups — and white women may not even recognize that the tension exists.

"For me, as an African-American woman, it means there are times when you know that the person doesn't have your back. You have to watch your back against a

---

33 Karen Kim in a discussion with the author.

white female," shared one black executive. Another said that white women want to be saviors. She noted that they will help women of color, but only on a limited basis and only if they get credit for doing the saving.

"It's complicated," said Tanya Odom, a bi-racial executive coach. "I think people often think [the relationship between white women and women of color] is better than it is."[34]

"The white female may not ever consider that women of color have twice the challenges," said Tonie Leatherberry, a senior executive at Deloitte.[35]

What makes the problems between white women and women of color so important is the relative success white women have had in the workplace. The numbers make it clear that white women are the frontrunners in the affirmative-action sweepstakes.

For instance, the *2005 Catalyst Member Benchmarking Report* states that white men made up 73 percent of senior executives in the organizations surveyed. This compared with a distant second of white women, at 18 percent, followed by a combined group of men of color at seven percent and a combined women-of-color group at two percent. Thus, while white women are not doing as well as one would expect if there were true workplace equity, they are doing markedly better than any other racial/

---

34 Tanya Odom interviewed by Ancella Livers, January 2012.
35 Tonie Leatherberry in a discussion with the author, January 5, 2012.

ethnic group. So much so that their presence at mid-to-senior levels dramatically outpaces women of color by four to one.[36]

It is clear that women of color are lagging behind in advancement opportunities. Thus, if white women don't recognize the power and influence they have in organizations and use it on behalf of themselves and other women, then the ability of women to help themselves seems greatly compromised.

Helayne Angelus of Kalypso (and a former executive with P&G) said, "As a white woman, I have been the beneficiary of affirmative action. White women now have a unique challenge to embrace their role to help women of color — African Americans, Latinas, Asians. This requires getting out of our comfort zones, understanding real differences in experiences and bridging those gaps."[37]

As stated earlier, ethno-bubbles do not affect only white women. Ethno/racial viewpoints also impact the perspectives of women of color and influence how they respond to and understand the experience of white women and other women of color.

"We talk at each other," said Regenia Stein. "That is white women's fault and women of color's fault."[38] Other

---

36 Catalyst, *2005 Catalyst Member Benchmarking Report*. http://www.catalyst.org/system/files/2005MemberBenchmarkingReport.pdf.

37 Helayne Angelus in an interview with Jenny Claggett, December 21, 2011.

38 Regenia Stein in a discussion with the author, January 11, 2012.

women agree, saying that the relationships between various groups of women are often distant.

For example, Karen Kim shared that making friends with African-American women can be difficult. She added that a friend of hers, another Asian-American woman, feels a disconnect with African-American culture and African-American women. "It's hard to break into it," Kim said. "No matter how much you feel like you're like them, or feel like them, it's closed."[39]

Throughout our research, a common truth became clear: Women are biased against other women, and that bias is getting in the way of women publically supporting other women. *And* it is also getting in the way of women serving as mentors to help more women succeed on a higher level.

In addition to this research, there are other societal expectations that may be coming into play. In the late 1970s, a term was coined for women who treated other women badly simply because they were women. It is called "The Queen Bee Syndrome." The Queen Bee Syndrome was first defined by G.L. Staines, T.E. Jayaratne, and C. Tavris in 1973, and describes a woman in a position of authority who views or treats subordinates more critically if they are female.[40] Have you experienced this, or have you seen it in your company?

---

39 Karen Kim in a discussion with the author.
40 G.L. Staines, T.E. Jayaratne, and C. Tavris, "The Queen Bee Syndrome." In *The Female Experience,* ed. C. Tavris. (Del Mar, CA: CRM Books, 1973).

Okay ladies, it's our time. What are we going to do? Are you willing to step out and have these courageous conversations? Are you open to becoming curious about our different paths?

CLEANING OUR OWN HOUSE TO CREATE OPPORTUNITY

"People think I am being biased when I support women. I am honestly concerned, as I don't want to be seen as just favoring women. It's a mindset. This is what causes women to not want to be seen as carrying the female banner. As a result, they overcompensate and don't support women in any visible way at all."[41] This is how Kim Smith, a senior executive with Texas Instruments, described what she felt was one of the primary reasons why women supporting other women is more complicated than what is seen on the surface.

Another piece of the complexity results from the reality that some of the women who have experienced success get to the top and then forget that someone helped them get there. It's like women get into this mental zone of thinking, "I have to lose in order for you to win," instead of "We *both* can win."

I think that, deep down, women feel inferior despite their success. And once a woman gets into a place of power, she doesn't want to do anything that would rock

---

41 Kim Smith in a discussion with the author, April 30, 2015.

the boat. This phenomenon is often referred to as the "Impostor Syndrome."[42]

The Impostor Syndrome is a feeling that you are somehow less deserving of success when compared to others. I recently saw this firsthand when I was coaching a white female executive that was so ready and so deserving of leading a business unit as a president. A talented, passionate individual known for getting results, she was VP of one of the functional units. The problem was, she didn't believe how deserving she was; she compared herself to everyone and everything, including the paper clips on her desk.

White women are willing to step into any job (yes, any job) without the experience or the know-how and guess what? The organization is supportive. Why? "Because they will grow into the job," is the typical response given by HR, supporters and sponsors. The point is they position themselves as being ready despite not having 100 percent of the capabilities. We need to realize that we have been stretching ourselves all of our lives to create the future we want for ourselves.

"White women haven't realized their power," said one of the senior executives I interviewed. "We are still trying to find our voice and build the confidence to ask for what we want."

---

42 Pauline Clance, Suzanne Imes, "The Imposter Phenomenon in High Achieving Women: Dynamics and Therapeutic Intervention," *Psychotherapy: Theory, Research and Practice* 15, no. 3 (1978).

WHAT IS THE SOLUTION?

"I think that a sense of security would help. I think more women would help if they realized, 'Oh, okay, you're not going to take my job. You are not my competition.' And perhaps even better might be the conversations we have with our daughters. I told my daughter that there is something you can learn and something you can teach with every person you interact with. All women need to work to plant the seed that women are allies and not competitors," said Marla Fielder, head of Pharmacy for the Houston/Dallas Marketplace for the Kroger Company.[43]

Women are not competing. We don't have enough critical mass to compete against each other. Yet women view each other as competition because society and the culture of corporate America are pitting women against each other. I remember when the second woman came on board as a member of the senior executive team when I was in corporate. The men immediately began comparing us, contrasting us and basically challenging us to prove who was stronger, tougher and more courageous. Unfortunately, we didn't realize what was going on and, unintentionally, we became enemies. We didn't do public battle, but there were subtle unspoken behaviors that suggested it was going to be her or me. I eventually left. And years after I left, she left, too. It was a lose/lose situation.

That doesn't have to be your story though.

---

43 Marla Fielder in a discussion with the author, July 13, 2015.

Things are clearer now. There is more research. While women have become more transparent in today's environment, we are not quite there. We need to build on the foundation and take it to a whole new level.

TIME FOR INSANE COURAGE

It's time for women to get some insane courage, the kind of courage that motivates them to step out with bold conviction no matter what. Most of us are hooked on the drug. What's the drug? Money, bennies, extras. I used to refer to them as the velvet handcuffs, not the golden handcuffs. (You know what I'm talking about.)

Back in the day, it was 100 percent health care coverage, private jets, first-class treatment. No matter where in the world you went, you were important — press coverage, limousines, pre-check-in for the hotel, the room according to your preferences, wine, beer or liquor of your choice in a fully stocked bar, room of your choice, the list goes on. Your team knew your likes and dislikes and it was their pleasure to please you.

Does anybody remember those days? They were not that long ago. Well, the truth is it is not that glamorous today — it never was that glamorous.

Are we paralyzed by the almighty dollar? The title? The recognition?

One of my friends shared this perspective, and I agree. In order for you to demonstrate courage, first and foremost, you have to be great. You can't step out and challenge the system if your own situation is less than buttoned up. So, let's not get the message twisted. We have to be solid in our own game and deliver the goods. I don't know one woman who wants to be held to a lower standard.

Courage comes from the confidence that you can and will deliver. You know that you are so good, your mindset is this: I am choosing to give my gifts and talents to this organization. I am employable anywhere, anytime.

Now what do you do with the power once you step out as a courageous supporter of women? Here's the first thing: Admit you don't know everything and get intentional about gaining new insight.

When was the last time you mentored someone who didn't look like you? When was the last time you had a meaningful and transparent conversation with a woman from a different generation than yours? What women come into your home? Do they all look like you? And let me really stretch you: How many women who don't look like you are you serving as their official or unofficial sponsor?

It's time for us to get intentional about getting to know one another. We can't drive the change that is needed if we can't support each other. And we can't support each other if we don't *know* each other.

The moment we become intentional and support each other is the moment we have created our *collective* voice, not our *competitive* voice.

COURAGEOUS CALL-TO-ACTION INITIATIVES

- Challenge yourself to become culturally competent, starting with gaining new knowledge about women and/or men who don't look like you. Be intentional about spending time outside of work in casual environments where you can get to know others that are not from your race.
- Participate in employee resource group sessions where you will be in the minority.
- Identify six women from different ethnicities and/or generations that you will commit to investing in for one full year.
- Develop the courage and confidence to ask the tough questions when you get a seat at the table. Ask questions like, "Can we diversify our candidate pool so that we have a broader representation?"
- Use your power. Start with your own team. What does your team look like? Would your team members say that you have created an "inclusive environment" where courageous conversations can happen anytime? Have you invested in your team's development of cultural competencies? Are you really able to lead by example?
- Have a special conversation with your sons and daughters about equality. Plant the seed early and nurture it throughout their lives.

- Write a legacy statement and ensure that part of your legacy is connected to opening the door for other women to achieve more success than you have.

Three

Courageous Conversations About Driving Your Own Equality

"Forget conventionalisms; forget what
the world thinks of you stepping out of
your place; think your best thoughts,
speak your best words, work your best
works, looking to your own
conscience for approval."

–Susan B. Anthony

When I wrote *Her Corner Office*, I wrote it for women. I wanted to give women a roadmap for finding their voice and place in corporate America. That book (now available in a second edition) offers a tremendous amount of tips, strategies and tools for *anyone* who is seriously interested in career success.

What I now realize, however, is that I should have written about more than strategies, tips and tools. I needed to also tie in the role that emotional intelligence plays in one's success. In this chapter, we will specifically focus on providing practical steps for self-advocacy and emotional intelligence.

SELF-ADVOCATE, STAND TALL AND ASK FOR WHAT YOU WANT

Each of us must know how to self-advocate. Self-advocacy is defined as the action of representing one's self or one's views or interests. If you don't advocate for yourself, the system will suck you up and spit you out, leaving you weak, second-guessing yourself and longing for a place where you can truly be accepted.

Here's the deal: We all must demand acceptance. We all must demand respect. And we all must send the proper signals to the world that we bring value.

"When we speak about our work, we need to use power words to explain the value of our work," shared Dr. Victoria Medvec, the Adeline Barry Davee professor of Management & Organizations at the Kellogg School of Management at Northwestern University.[44]

I participated in a session that she led a few years ago where 35 senior executive women were present. She asked each woman to stand and introduce herself. She

---

44 Victoria Medvec in a discussion with the author, July 2016.

didn't share, however, that she was grading each person's self-advocacy capabilities and their use of appropriate power words to describe their work. Out of the 35 women, only two women were credited for being able to self-advocate. Yes, I said two.

One is a friend who is the Senior Vice President and General Merchandise Manager responsible for leading merchandising strategies for the baby, chemicals, paper goods, over-the-counter and optical departments for Walmart stores in the United States. She leads a $40 billion business. The second executive is also a friend, the Senior Vice President and Chief Customer Officer at PepsiCo. She leads a $10 billion business.

Each of them used words and phrases like "I lead," "under my leadership," "the team that I lead," "the direction that I have set," or "the strategy I have built serves to drive (X) business which represents (%) of the company's business."

What's the point?

The two women Victoria deemed capable of self-advocating knew the connection between their work, their team's work and the organization.

Are you capable of presenting your work in this manner? Can you outline the value correlation between your work and your organization's goals? Do you know what percentage of the company's annual sales revenue your work contributes to? These are questions every one of us must think about.

To create your own path to success you must know your value. You must know yourself.

Success starts from the inside out — you must respect yourself if you want others to respect you. You must be clear about what you want and how to get there. If you are expecting someone to come and give it to you, it will never happen.

So, before we can talk about stepping out to build allies or serve the organization as agents of change, we must take time to make sure that you can *stand tall*. Standing tall means you have confidence in your own abilities. Standing tall means you trust yourself.

If you are reading this and the itty-bitty pity committee of self-doubt is suggesting you aren't as confident as you should be, don't worry. There's good news. Confidence is not something that you are born with, but it *can* be developed. People with low self-esteem don't trust themselves, so they need validation outside themselves. My challenge to myself and to you is to be intentional about making deposits into your spirit bank to build your confidence and your mental toughness.

Stepping out as an agent of change to drive equality will place you in situations of conflict. It just does. Any time anyone presses forward to advance an agenda, there will be conflict. Because of socialization, women and many people of color tend to shy away from conflict and discomfort. Any person who is a part of a minority group might be more hesitant to draw attention to himself or herself for fear of being misinterpreted or chastised for stepping out of their designated role.

My husband's Aunt Julie is a psychiatrist and one of nine children born to Ernest and Myrtle Ponquinette. She was the first African-American female to attend Spring Hill College, a Jesuit institution in Mobile, Alabama, in 1956. I sat down with her to gain a better appreciation of how she stepped out and stood tall to be the first, pressing on in the spite of rejection and racism.

She told me women need to get super clear about what they want and have the confidence and courage within them to try new things. Essentially, they just need to step out of their comfort zone.

"No one ever told me I couldn't be a doctor," she shared. "I told *myself* I could be a doctor. When rejection reared its ugly head, I told myself to stay focused."

"Sheryl Sandberg wrote a book called *Lean In*. Are you familiar with it?" I asked. She nodded while I continued, "Her book speaks to the importance of confidence. She suggests that women need to stop second-guessing themselves."

Julie responded by saying, "Let me tell you about an article entitled *Confidence of Champions* by Chris Kanyane. This is something every woman should read."

"Why?" I asked.

"Because it truly explains where confidence comes from," she stated. "You have to believe inside if you want to achieve anything. For me, I leaned on the confidence that my family had in my capabilities and, of course, my faith. If you are a woman of color, you have confidence and faith. I don't know many women who, like Ms. Sandberg, were afforded very powerful connections and relationships so early in her life. I was secure in my family support.

That support enabled me to take the risk I needed to be the first."

"And by the way, Trudy," she continued, "as you very well know, many women are still pressing on and 'becoming the first.' Women of all shades — and men, too. But since you are focused on women, let me say this. Women struggle to see the value of the relationship they have with themselves. We need to have the right mindset. To achieve the right mindset, we have to get quiet and develop the capability to trust ourselves."[45]

Is your mindset right? Do you trust yourself? Are you clear about your life vision and career vision? Are you showing up in a way that allows you to build a path to getting what you want? Are you willing to take risks that can propel you to personal and professional fulfillment? Do you have a career strategy? If you can't answer these questions definitively, then you've got some thinking to do.

Aunt Julie's insight reminded me of a lady who could answer yes to all of these questions and more.

Delia.

Delia is an uber-intelligent research scientist, technology strategist and program manager. She holds doctorate and master's degrees in industrial and systems engineering with specializations in human factors engineering and management systems engineering. Her undergraduate degree is in mechanical engineering.

---

45 Julie Joyner in a discussion with the author, August 20, 2012.

Over the past decade, Delia has served as a loyal change agent and key contributor to strategy for a giant global technology company. She has a stellar Fortune 200 track record of driving large-scale technology change that enhances competitive position, revenues and market share. But Delia went through a very difficult time a few years back. Here's what happened:

In 2010 Delia's team underwent a reorganization and Delia was transferred to a different unit. At first, everything seemed fine. She meshed well with her colleagues and her new boss. But soon, this new manager revealed himself to be a tyrant and a control freak. Why the sudden resistance, she wondered. Others appreciated her work and noticed her intelligence and value. Outside consultants loved her.

Delia's work life soon became a living hell. Her new manager micromanaged her, he publicly argued with her decisions, and when she would ask for feedback, his responses were vague. What was the problem? Unbeknownst to Delia, this new manager had a small group of male cohorts with whom he wanted to surround himself. He had not been successful in securing all his buddies to his group during the reorg, so his plan was to drive Delia out so he could make his team complete. Ever heard of *cronyism*? This is exactly what was happening to Delia.

Eventually, Delia decided she'd had enough. Within two weeks of making her decision, she had a new job thanks to her vast network. After she left this dysfunctional situation, her manager slammed her during her last performance appraisal. But Delia, confident in her skills and determined to stand up for herself, went to HR and secured backing for the poor management of her review. When HR approached the manager, he eventually rewrote the appraisal. Delia now feels complete in her new position.

Maybe you haven't had a bad manager yet. If you haven't, hold on, your day is coming. Thriving in corporate America requires mental toughness. People will push you. They will challenge your work. They will challenge your capabilities. You must stand tall knowing who you are and what you stand for. People will treat you however you allow them to treat you.

KNOW YOURSELF AND OWN YOUR STORY

Kathleen Kelley Reardon, in a *Harvard Business Review* article, suggests that, "Every person is at least 75 percent responsible for how others treat them." [46]

Let that soak in for a minute.

Why do we tolerate bad behavior? Why don't we say something? What kind of advice would *you* have given Delia if she was someone you cared about? Of course, you would have been outraged, but then maybe your outrage would have turned to fear, which would cause you to advise Delia to just suck it up and get over it.

---

46 Kathleen Kelley Reardon, "7 Things to Say When a Conversation Turns Negative," *Harvard Business Review,* May 11, 2016.

Have you ever heard sayings like, "Put on your big girl panties or big guy shorts?" We must know what we value, and we must know what we will not tolerate. And we really need to think of these things *before* we start our careers and be willing to constantly reevaluate them.

But honestly, when we get out of college, we are moved to instantly get a job — I'll take any job, just pay me! We got caught up in the hype of starting our careers, seeking the briefcase, business cards, company credit card and employer-paid smartphone.

What were we thinking?

So many people, especially women, as addressed in the infamous 2012 *Atlantic* article "Why Women Still Can't Have It All" by Anne-Marie Slaughter, assert that there is no way we can ever have it all. I applaud her for calling out what we all know: The business world does not treat women fairly. We have known this is true for decades.

A study in the *Work, Employment and Society Journal* discovered that women are paid less and their jobs are less flexible and more stressful than men's jobs. They also have fewer opportunities for advancement. Researchers say the results disprove the theory that women have *voluntarily* traded the chance at high-powered jobs in order to gain more flexibility for their responsibilities at home.[47] Additionally, addressing racial inequality, according to

---

47 Haya Stier, Meir Yaish. "Occupational Segregation and Gender Inequality and Job Quality: A Multi-Level Approach," *Work, Employment and Society* 28, no. 2, (2014).

Equal Employment Opportunity Commission Chair Jenny R. Yang, "Race constitutes 35 percent of all discrimination charges filed under the statutes the EEOC enforces, which also cover discrimination because of age, disability, and family medical history or genetic information."[48] Even though the number of people of color in senior-level positions has risen significantly since the EEOC started tracking this data in 1966, racial discrimination remains a significant problem.

I heard Indra Nooyi share her best piece of career advice several years back while attending a women's leadership conference. Her comments didn't truly hit home until later, and they have since stuck with me. She said women need to "marry well." It still doesn't sit perfectly with me, but there is something to what she is saying.

I remember, just after our first child was born, Mike and I would go to bed at the same time and would watch TV to unwind before going to sleep. One night when we got in bed, Mike started talking about this great movie that was coming on that he wanted to watch. He tried to talk me into staying up to see the movie too.

"I can't," I said. "Adam will be waking up for his feeding at 2 a.m."

As I started going to sleep, I clearly remember feeling miffed, thinking to myself, *You get to watch a movie,*

48 Jenny Yang, "Job Discrimination Still a Challenge," Editorial. *Miami Herald* (Miami, FL), July 1, 2015. http://www.miamiherald.com/opinion/op-ed/article26010319.html.

and I can't because I am the one taking care of the baby. Seriously? It was a wake-up call.

The next day, Mike and I had a heart-to-heart conversation. He is a really good man and an excellent father, but I needed a *full* partner. What I realized in that moment of discovering my own truth is that I hadn't ever asked him, with intention, to share the responsibilities for our child, as in getting up in the middle of the night to feed the baby. To take his turn, so to speak. And when I did, he responded and committed.

Women need to stop taking on all the responsibility for themselves *and* everyone else. And if we have married well, we have a partner just waiting for an invitation to the responsibility of caring for children.

Okay, I know you are probably saying to yourself, "I shouldn't have to ask him." I said that to myself as well. But that wasn't working that well for me. And I'll bet it's not working for you. You have the right to ask for what you need, so have the meeting. Speak the truth about your needs.

I recently led a group coaching session for 10 married women with children who were Senior Directors and Vice Presidents. There were three main themes that came out through during our discussion: work/life balance, navigating an organization's culture in an authentic way and engaging with the senior leadership team as a thought leader.

I began our session by asking some fundamental questions:

1. What is your vision for serving as a mother?
2. What is your vision for your role as a wife?
3. When was the last time you had a family meeting to discuss rules and responsibilities?
4. What steps have you taken to ensure that you and your family members stay on the right track?

To my surprise, none of the 10 women present had a vision they could state for their role as a mother or as a wife. None of them were engaging in family meetings focused on rules and responsibilities. As a result, none of them could offer a recap of any steps they had taken to keep their families on the right course.

No wonder they were frustrated. No wonder they felt like they were exhausted. No wonder their emotions were running out of control. They didn't have a plan or a strategy. You can't expect the picture you want to create to just appear out of thin air; you have to do the work. Goals, strategies and plans do succeed, but only when you put in the work.

I know it is difficult to create your own path and defy the odds, but it *is* possible. Maybe we can't have it all at the same time, but I believe that if we know ourselves, defend our values and get really bold in our decisions, we can create a path to success.

I love the Cathy Englebert philosophy of "You *can* have it all!" In an interview by Lillian Cunningham in the March 20, 2015 edition of *The Washington Post*, Cathy Englebert spoke out on becoming Deloitte's first female CEO and addressed female success in the workplace.

When Cathy started her career 30 years ago, there were very few women in the accounting world. Today, Cathy is the first female CEO of the organization. In addition to sharing her prioritization (family first, job second), she was asked about the biggest barriers to success for women.

This was her response:

"The biggest barrier for women is the thought that they can't have it all. Can they have a high-performing career? Can they have a career that evolves with the way our clients evolve? And can they raise children, or take care of elderly parents, or whatever issue they have in their personal life? That, I believe, is still the impediment.

"We have got to give ourselves permission to say that we can have it all, and we are willing to do what it takes to make sure of it.

"I was pregnant with my first child the year I was up for partner. I started to think to myself, 'Can I actually do this?' I even looked at a job opportunity outside the firm. It was really difficult for me to make that decision, to stay or to go. There's a level of uncertainty when you think about the future, when you think about the job you have today, and then wonder if you can balance it all."[49]

We all must learn to trust our inner voice. Silence the itty-bitty pity committee of self-doubt. There is no

---

49 Lillian Cunningham, "Cathy Engelbert on Becoming Deloitte's First Female CEO," *Washington Post*, (Washington, D.C.) March 20, 2015.

apology needed from any of us for wanting to bring our talents to bear. Organizations need us to add value. They need us to contribute at our highest levels. As Dr. Joyner said, "You have to speak to yourself. You must believe in yourself."

Ana's story proves what I am saying to be true.

Ana (she asked us not to use her last name) is a smart woman from Brazil. She has an undergraduate and master's degree in chemical engineering, along with her Ph.D. Oh, and did I mention she holds more than 60 patents? She is a rock star. But this rock star stumbled in corporate America and needed to learn how to develop her own strategy for success, starting with her mindset. She shared her story with me.

"I wasn't accepted," she said. "My managers often joked about my English. Although I speak three languages, they made me second-guess myself. On top of that, the senior leaders gave the good projects to men who were members of the dominant group."[50]

Realize that the dominant group can shift depending upon your organization. In this case, the dominant group was white men. In today's workforce, the dominant group can be Asian men, Indian men and even white women, depending on where you work. We will talk about this dynamic in more detail later in the book.

---

50 Ana (she chose not to use last name) in a discussion with the author.

"I feel isolated," she said, tears welling in her eyes. "I try to act like the guys to obtain the reward I think I deserve, but it is not working. I am not getting anywhere. I want to be a principal engineer. When I started at this company, I believed that I could do it. But they have made me feel inadequate."

"What?" I exclaimed. "What are you talking about? Are you giving your power away? Do you think that they are in control, or are you in control?"

"I don't know who is in charge," she answered.[51]

"That's the problem," I told her. "*You* are in charge. You are in charge, and you must believe that you are in charge of stepping out as the architect of your own future. It all starts with your mindset. And remember, power not used will evaporate over time."

I continued by teaching her about a *fixed mindset* versus a *growth mindset*. If you will remember from Chapter 1 of this book, mindset is a simple idea discovered by Stanford University psychologist Carol Dweck that demonstrates that a person's mindset, either fixed or growth, can determine their success in reaching for goals. In a fixed mindset, people believe certain qualities, such as intelligence or talent, are static and unchangeable. But in a growth mindset, people believe that these same qualities can be developed through dedication and practice.

"So, Ana, where do you stand?" I asked. "Are you in the fixed or growth mindset?" Tears began to roll down

---

51 Ibid.

her cheeks. "Don't worry," I said as I tried to comfort her. "It is important that you recognize your starting point. Now we get to talk about choices. You have a choice. You don't have to act like anyone else. You don't have to pretend to be someone you are not. You don't have to be comfortable with getting projects that rob your energy."

I asked her to do a "defining moments" map. She asked what that was.

"It is a recap of your life to date. What you have been through and what you have learned about yourself. It is the most powerful tool to help you realize your value. Limit the defining moments to 10 on the first go-round."

I shared how this exercise taught me that I am an agent of change: To believe in yourself, you must know yourself. And knowing yourself is critical to showing up in an authentic way. When you show up authentically, you can perform at your very best. It is where your brilliance lies.

Tapping in to who you are requires you to look at the good, the bad and the ugly.

The point I made to Ana and I make to you is that you have a choice. You don't have to sit in a position that doesn't align with your values, doesn't give you energy, doesn't play to your strengths and doesn't empower you to create your own equality.

"Women don't naturally play big," says Tara Mohr, author of *Playing Big: Find Your Voice, Your Mission, Your Message*. In the book, Tara admits that playing small was one of her own struggles. In her coaching practice, she began to notice a pattern of women playing small. She was seeing women who were talented, full of ideas and aspiration, but didn't see their own brilliance. She wanted to understand why the women were holding back. They were shrinking instead of taking up space as confident, bold leaders.

To validate her observations, she sent out a survey with a list of challenges that women typically face. It included work/life balance, stress, not enough time, financial problems, health challenges and relationship issues.

But because of the patterns she observed, she added one more challenge to the list: *I'm playing small.*

When the survey responses came back, *I'm playing small* was what the largest number of women deemed as their most significant problem.

This was a very interesting finding as it suggests that we, women of all colors and backgrounds, know that we are not living up to our greatest potential.

Women are socialized to criticize themselves. We are socialized to cover.

Covering is an idea explored by the Chief Justice Earl Warren Professor of Constitutional Law at the NYU School of Law, Professor Kenji Yoshino. He found the term while researching 20th-century sociologist Erving Goffman.

Goffman coined the term *covering* to describe how we all "modulate our identities in order to be accepted by the mainstream." In his book *Covering: The Hidden Assault on Our Civil Rights*, Yoshino argues that the demand to cover can pose a hidden threat to our civil rights. He writes the book through the lens of a gay Asian male and shares personal stories that are both moving and convicting.

We all cover, he says. But women and people of color cover more often in an attempt to be accepted by the dominant group. We cover on four axes: association, affiliation, appearance and advocacy.

"Covering," Yoshino says, "is a strategy through which an individual downplays a known stigmatized identity to blend into the mainstream. Covering excises a tax on a person's engagement, energy and innovation. Sixty-one percent report covering on at least one axis (including Caucasian and Asian men), but some people pay a higher tax than others, especially gay, female and black cohorts."[52]

We all need to stop trying to be someone we are not. If you have never been able to give a name to behavior that is not authentic, you have it now. Each of us is going to need to be willing to use our power and influence to make equality become a reality. The price of covering is too high. It compromises our brilliance and leaves us exhausted and longing for cultures where we are accepted for who we are, period!

If we agree that covering robs us of showing up authentically, then we must also agree that finding the courage to create a new future requires women, people of color and those in the LGBT community to stop covering.

---

52 Kenji Yoshino, *Covering: The Hidden Assault on Our Civil Rights* (New York: Random House, 2006).

How can a woman or person of color survive trying to be someone they are not? How can we deny our heritage?

My husband and I are both brown-skinned creoles who are not necessarily liked by light-skinned creoles. It is an interesting dynamic, this racism that exists between members of the same culture.

Mike and I have been married for 36 years. When we got married, we didn't know there was bad blood that existed behind the scenes between our families. Growing up in Mobile, Alabama, where light creoles were viewed as smarter and better, was a real annoyance on top of the true racism we experienced. It was, nonetheless, impactful in a negative way.

My mother didn't come to our wedding. It was a painful experience for me. My curiosity pushed me to try to understand why a mother wouldn't be there for her own daughter's wedding. Well, as it turns out, when my mother was young, she was actually a nursemaid for my husband's grandfather, Ambrose Parker, for whom my younger sister Amberosine is named.

I know, complicated, right?

Well, while under their employ, my mother was rejected by my in-laws — particularly my husband's grandmother — for being too dark. When my mother showed up for her nursing duties, she was relegated to enter the house by the back door. And you know what? She did it. She acquiesced. She was covering. It was the only way to advance her agenda of care. It was more important to my mother to serve than to be served. She eventually came to terms with her own truth, demanding to be respected as a beautiful brown creole without apology.

I am grateful to her for showing me how to stand in my authenticity and show up in a way that says to the world, "I am present. Hear me and watch me contribute to making things better for you and for me."

Bias was extremely visible, and no one other than creoles were involved. As I have said, bias is something we all have. The question, then, is how does that bias serve you? And are you willing, in a growth mindset, to take on new biases that serve you better?

"It takes a personal strategy to not cover," offered Rhonda Mims, a black woman and Managing Director of Corporate Social Responsibility at Paul Hastings.

"Growing up in Georgia, my parents knew that I would face biases being a strong woman of color who wanted to one day run an organization in the CEO seat. They taught me to see the bias and move beyond it. I know that it is there. Anyone who doesn't admit that organizations are filled with leaders who are biased is not telling the truth," shared Rhonda.[53]

To create a new future, we must embrace our current reality, exactly where we started in Chapter 1. There is no way to move forward significantly if the truth can't be admitted.

"For me, I compartmentalize. I acknowledge that biases and other more direct factors get in my way, but I

---

53 Rhonda Mims in a discussion with the author, March 21, 2015.

am determined to build a wall around it. By compartmentalizing, it goes to the back of my mind. It helps me to process every experience through a lens of possibility versus a lens of limitations. I have learned to compartmentalize very well. In any given situation, I ask, 'Is this reality? How do I cope with this?' Then I decide if it's my issue or if it's their issue. If it's their issue, I'm going to move around it. I refuse to let it stop me," Rhonda stated.

She continued, "Women need to take on and internalize every step of the way. I spend a lot of time strategizing in my head. I try to play out each scenario, career-wise. I'm thoughtful about each step, but I don't focus on it every day. I am sure to deliver on my day-to-day job, but I always strategize on next steps. I hope other women of color have figured this out. Plus, I have a board of advisors. You must have a board of advisors, trusted people of all races, from whom you gain insight. I reach out to them informally, not all at one time," she said.[54]

Rhonda's point is spot on — you must have a strategy.

A critical component of the strategy has to be developing enterprise relationships. Trust me when I say that your career aspirations will never materialize if you stay in a cube or an office all day. You must get out and talk to people. You've got to create some energy by sharing who you are. But to share who you are you have to own your story. You have to embrace your responsibility as the author of your life.

---

54 Ibid.

This is true whether we are talking about your personal *or* professional aspirations. In one of the experiential learning sessions that the Center for Workforce Excellence offers for organizations that are trying to build a workforce that mirrors the face of the consumer at every level, we utilize two very powerful exercises. In pursuit of creating your own level playing field, I encourage you to use these in building your own strategy. The first exercise is the defining moments map exercise I shared with Ana earlier in this chapter. The spin we put on that exercise is this: We ask people to draw out their map by highlighting defining moments, such as those experiences that have had major impact upon your values and belief system. These moments shape your character and leadership constitution. In the second piece, we ask participants to look for what they did in their lives to help lead themselves and others. We ask participants to ask themselves how these experiences helped shape their worldview.

Recently while I was being interviewed, the interviewer asked me about these exercises; specifically, what to do once you have insight on these defining experiences.

I smiled and said, "That's where the magic happens. You take these experiences and reflect on what leadership capability or trait was created. Then you reflect on how this capability supports your leadership perspective and finally you outline how this perspective affects your leadership impact."

I continued with this example: In the movie *Beasts of No Nation*, the opening scene shows a family being torn apart. The rebels are overtaking the city. The village is at war. The men are separated from the children. The mother of one family is holding a small baby. She is pushed into a car. Her other children are crying for her, but she can only take one child.

As the scene progresses, the men, including a young boy played by Abraham Nii Attah, are taking refuge, trying to hide from the rebels. One of the family members actually carries the grandfather on his back because he can't walk. Despite their efforts, the rebels catch the men and kill them.

As the chaos continues, the little boy escapes into the jungle. He is alone and hears strange sounds but doesn't know where the sounds are coming from. He cannot see anything or anyone. He is captured and begins a life as a child soldier.[55]

That is a defining life experience.

Because of this experience, he develops his resilience. Little did he know how much he would have to rely on his resilience to survive the things that would happen later in his life.

We can't change the experiences we have had; neither should we want to. There is something to learn from every experience. And in learning it, we are made stronger and

---

55 Cary Joji Fukunaga, *Beasts of No Nation*, Film, Directed by Cary Joji Fukunaga (2015; Venice: Red Crown Productions, Primary Productions, Parliament of Owls, Bleeker Street, Netflix, 2015.), Film and streaming.

better equipped to step out and show the world who we are — for real.

You are stronger than you think. You just have to go deep to find out what you are made of and then your own story will come out.

GET A SEAT AT THE TABLE (AND KEEP IT)

If you are willing to deploy the strategies that put you in the driver's seat to control your own destiny, you will rise to the level when you are invited to take a seat at the table.

You know the table — the power table where all the decision-makers of the company sit, regardless of why or how they got there. Lots of interesting things happen at the power table; people's lives are shaped at this table, which reminds me of something my dear friend Rosalind Hudnell shared.

"Women need to recognize that their place at the table is waiting for them and they need to step up and claim the seat, that's first," said Rosalind. "Once you get a seat at the table, don't get up until you have gotten everything you came to get. The seat is not just for you. Your agenda needs to be bigger than you. Women need to ask themselves, 'Why am I at this table? What am I advancing in terms of an agenda?' Sometimes women and people of color think they don't deserve the seat, and others believe that it is a seat they shouldn't have."

She continued, "We must realize that we worked so hard to get the seat, but what got us there is not going to keep us there. We need to start to relax and eagerly embrace the empowerment that awaits us. Believe me when I say you have the power. It is all about the shopper's purse. And in this nation and across the world, women rule."[56]

I have seen a lot of women and people of color become paranoid that their seat might be taken away from them any day. You can almost see the fear in their eyes. When this happens, they become paralyzed, and from that moment on, their seat is useless. Their power is no longer real.

I have also seen women get to the top and become arrogant. We stop taking risks, as Rosalind said, that will help us and help the company. It's a tragedy to end up in either camp.

"Instead, women need to get to the top and use their power to make a difference for others, women *and* men. But especially for other women. And here's what I really want your readers to know," Rosalind said as she leaned in closer to me. "Once you do get a seat at the table, don't get up until you have achieved everything that you intended to get!"

Touché.

---

56 Rosalind Hudnell in a discussion with the author, May 18, 2015.

COURAGEOUS CALL-TO-ACTION REFLECTION QUESTIONS

- Have you taken the time and made the effort to define your life vision? Your career vision? Your career strategy? Do you revisit these on a regular basis and update them?
- Do you self-advocate? Define your value as it relates to your team and organization.
- What or who is your support system? Whom do you call on when your self-confidence gets shaken? Whom do you personally support and help build up?
- Look at your own organization. Can you identify men or women in leadership roles who really encourage individuals and help mentor and shape minorities into leadership roles themselves? Are you on their radar screen? Why or why not?

Four

Courageous Conversations
About the Role of Men

"Men are still 85% of senior leadership
in most companies. This means they are
the greatest problem…and the greatest
opportunity for a solution. You will never
drive long-term systemic change for
women without active
male engagement."

— JEFFERY TOBIAS HALTER, PRESIDENT OF
YWOMEN

Over the years, I have had countless conversations with business leaders, chief diversity officers and human resources officers about what it will take to move the needle on diversity and inclusion.

In a recent conversation with a female leader who had stepped into a diversity and inclusion leadership role, she asked me, "Why hasn't more been accomplished in embedding diversity and inclusion?"

I responded, "One of the biggest obstacles that stands in the way of achieving gender equality is a lack of total engagement and ownership on the part of men. It is also one of the biggest opportunities." It's not that men don't see or understand the demographic shifts in America and throughout the rest of the world, it's that they must become sensitive to the culture changes taking place throughout their organizations. They must process these changes on an emotional level. It has to become personal. I find it is interesting that men, mainly white men, will act like they have knowledge of things even when they know absolutely nothing. So, what is the problem? Why is it when it comes to diversity and inclusion and equality, they suddenly lack confidence, become less assured of themselves and disengage?

"The problem," I continued, "is that men, particularly white men, see diversity as a threat to their power. They are not looking to correct the wrongs that rob the business world of engagement from all employees. They are thinking about loss, and it is very scary. We have to help them recognize that there are personal and professional benefits to completely buying in. And I think we must acknowledge that they don't know how to come out as ambassadors. They would never say this, but I believe they are paralyzed by fear."

"Why is there so much fear on the part of the dominant group?" she asked.

"It's change. Change brings about fear no matter what the subject. And I think European-descended white men have yet to take ownership of their own diversity, meaning most white men come from a diverse heritage, whether it's Irish, German, French, or multicultural. When they *do* take ownership, the scales are removed from their eyes and they form a different worldview," I shared. "But, as with any change effort, there are some who will never believe."

MAKING IT PERSONAL

Don Knauss is a very accomplished businessman. Before he retired he was CEO of Clorox. He now serves on a number of boards including Target and Kellogg. Don has a personal moment that convinced him he needed to stand for equality. It happened years ago when he was young in his career. Don and his wife were a young, dual-income family raising their children and dealing with all the pressures related to managing the stresses of life. One day his wife came home and shared a story that changed his perspective about equality, particularly equality of pay. She shared that during a conversation with her male colleagues, she found out she wasn't making the same compensation as they were for doing the same job. She was hurt, disappointed, and wanted to do something about it. When she told Don, he insisted she go back to work the next morning and speak to her manager and the human resource officer. She did. She approached her manager about her concerns. He asked her why she was complaining and said, "You have a husband. These men are the bread winners of their families and they need their money. You can understand that. "I am doing the same job," she responded. "I should get paid exactly what they get paid." To which her manager replied, "There is nothing I can do. Take it up with HR."

She approached HR, shared her story, and asked if the company endorsed men and women not being paid the same for doing the same job. The HR representatives simply said to her that salary increases were offered at the recommendation of the manager and that they would look into it. Her frustrations only became more intense. She felt like no one would listen. She went home that night and shared with Don the responses she obtained from trying to be treated fairly. His response speaks volumes about the power of a man deciding to make it personal when issues of equality and equal treatment are called into question. He told his wife to quit. "Find another job," he said. "And make sure you ask about pay. This is not right."

As a result of this very personal experience, Don became a public champion for equal treatment for men and women. He went on to sponsor women's employee resource groups. He was one of the first men to provide seed money to what is now known as the Network of Executive Women. He became bold and intentional. He found conviction around his passion. He recognized that he needed to get involved and he did. We need more of these leaders to take interest in the inequalities that exist in the business world. The easiest thing to do is simply to say that it is not your problem. If you are truly a leader, then you cannot be silent. You must follow Don's lead and take action.[57]

If you have been around me for any length of time during the last 17 years, you have heard this story, so forgive me. I need to tell it again because it is a demonstration of the power of men who believe in equality. Early in my career I had the privilege of meeting a man by the name of James White. A lady that I met at a training course, Polly Dolan, connected the two of us. At the time of the introduction, James and I were both at the Director level. He was working for a company called Purina Pet Care, now Nestlé Purina Pet Care. I was working for Brown and Williamson. James and I began a relationship as reciprocal mentors to each other. Both our careers continued to accelerate. James was a pioneer in creating employee resource groups for Purina Pet Care. He created an African-American group and then followed up by creating a women's leadership employee resource group.

Along the way James invited me several times to present to each of these groups. I was honored to share my thoughts. He was impressed with the clarity I offered on how to navigate corporate America as a minority or a woman. Well, time passed. James got promoted. I got promoted. We both became VPs and then James was promoted to an SVP. It was about that time that I made the decision to leave corporate America. I had this crazy idea

---

57 Don Knauss in a discussion with the author.

that I would change corporate America into a place where every employee was welcomed, valued and afforded equal opportunities to thrive.

When I shared with a small group of friends, including Polly Dolan, that I was leaving corporate America, Polly shared it with James. I remember flying home from Louisville, Kentucky, on a Friday. I literally cried the entire way home from Louisville to Dallas. All kinds of thoughts ran through my head. The fear of the future dominated my thoughts in a big way. But I knew that I was supposed to help other people experience career success. I just thought it would happen when I was 50. God decided it would happen at 41. It was 2001. As it turned out it was not a good time to start a business. We all remember what happened on September 11, 2001, with the terrorist attacks in New York, Washington, D.C., and Pennsylvania.

James called me that next Monday. He wanted to know if I would like to consider working for Purina Pet Care. I was flattered, but shared with James that I wanted to help make corporate America a better place for women and people of color. He was not surprised by my decision, but he challenged me to think about the impact a woman of color at the VP level would have upon the consumer goods industry. I was touched by his confidence. But I knew I needed to be in a space where I could tell the truth about bias, privilege, racism, sexism, and my experience with some members of the dominant group.

We engaged in a long conversation about culture, leadership, and the changes that I thought needed to occur. He asked me to take a couple of days to think about how we could work together. He believed in the power of diversity and inclusion before the word "inclusion" was a buzz word. He took bold stances within his company and in the industry about leveling the playing field for women and people of color. He called me three days later. He asked again if I was sure that I wanted to coach, train and do all the other things I had shared with him. I held firm behind my conviction. He responded by saying, "I have six women who I believe can accelerate to the C-suite." He shared that he believed it was important to get more women into leadership positions in order to create cultures where everyone was valued, the consumer's voice was represented, and innovation could thrive. As you can see he was a man ahead of his time. He made the decision to invest in these women. He called out the fact that the company didn't have female leaders in the sales division. He spoke possibility into the spirits of these women. He mentored and sponsored these women. He stood in traffic when other leaders were questioning why he was focusing on females and people of color. He was courageous. He was bold and still is.

I am happy to report that five of those six women are now in the C-suite at various organizations. They are adding value and shaping their organizations in ways they didn't imagine. James has never lost his desire to right the ship. He went onto become the CEO of Jamba Juice. Today he and two colleagues have created a nonprofit called the Director's Academy that is focused on getting more women and multicultural leaders onto board appointments. He is a role model for equality. What did he do that most men don't do? He invested in the future of women and people of color. He used his power to give the non-dominant leaders cover so they could make mistakes without it representing the end of their career. He refused to remain blind to inequalities. Are you willing to invest in women and people of color? Are you willing to step out and identify talent that doesn't look like you? Are you bold enough to demonstrate behaviors that send the signal that you believe in the power of inclusion? Are you willing to serve the organization you work for and the world as a change agent and an early adopter of equality? Do you lead with a mindset that every employee deserves equal rights to opportunities?[58]

THE IMPORTANCE OF TRUE ENLIGHTENMENT

My husband, Mike, retired from television production after spending 37 years of his life dedicated to living out his passion. During his last job in Dallas, Texas, he worked with a gentleman who was in his thirties who would constantly and proudly boast that his grandfather was an active leader in the Ku Klux Klan. Mike would share his frustration about this gentleman with me, and I would try to assure him that no one in his right mind would boast about such a thing. Mike wholeheartedly disagreed.

---

58 James White in a discussion with the author.

"I think he does it to see if he can stir me up," Mike replied.

"So how do you respond? What do you say to him in the moment when he talks about the bad things his grandfather would do?" I asked.

"I look at him like he is crazy and walk away," Mike responded.

As he shared this experience with me for the tenth time, I am thinking in my head that this young man hasn't been enlightened. He doesn't get it. He has made a choice to buy into what his grandfather taught him — hook, line and sinker. He is not open. This type of person isn't worth you or me trying to convince to become an ally.

We must stay focused on the people who demonstrate a willingness to listen and learn. It hurts me to say that there are people who don't care about the feelings of others, but these people exist. And you know what? We work with some of them. But it doesn't mean we need to spend our energy trying to convince them of something they will never believe.

In my heart, I believe most men want to do the right thing, but I know there will be men who will not get on board. To those leaders, we say that we respectfully choose not to engage with you.

There are some men who have had life experiences that shaped them to view inequalities from a very personal stance. Last year, I met a white man who is a perfect example of the kind of person I am talking about.

Let's call him Mark. Mark is a very accomplished gentleman who runs a global organization for a Fortune 50 company. He sponsored a woman of color — we will call her Lisa — to be coached by me. Mark's boss is also a white male who supported Lisa's professional growth.

Mark's support went well beyond a superficial signature of a budget line. He wanted to speak to me to understand how Lisa was engaging in her development, specifically wanting to know if she was taking full ownership for her blind spots and if she was open to working on them.

In preparation for my conversation with him, I checked Mark's bio online and found the usual, a recap of a highly successful white male. Curiosity got the best of me so I asked Karen, my assistant, to set up time with Mark specifically to discuss his own boss. Fortunately, I have a really great relationship with Mark and he has a total servant leader's heart.

I started the conversation by asking, "What is the motivation behind your boss's support for Lisa?"

"He is a good guy, born in the Pittsburgh area to a large family," responded Mark. "His parents had 11 children. His parents were Catholic and raised the family in that faith. He grew up on the wrong side of the tracks, so he knows how it feels to be poor, to be marginalized. He gets it. He gets what Lisa is going through to prove herself to the leaders who will ultimately decide her future."

"That helps tremendously," I shared. "I feel much more prepared now to engage with him."

The call with Mark's boss was scheduled to be 15 minutes long. We ended up talking for 45 and could have gone on another 45 minutes more. I started the call by explaining to him that we had a tremendous amount in common though we had never met.

"How so?" he asked.

"We are both from large families. We were both raised Catholic. And we both know the negative impact of being judged as less-than," I said.

He was quick with his response, "What do you mean?"

Oh no, I thought, *maybe it wasn't such a good idea to try and connect with him on such a deeply personal level.*

"Well," I said, "I understand from talking to Lisa and Mark that you experienced some challenges growing up with being accepted. And so did I. I bring that up because I want to set some context for Lisa's challenges. I don't want to offer apologies, but it is important for her key stakeholders to understand the barriers that she faces on a daily basis."

To my surprise, he replied, "The world sees me as a white male who is very successful. In fact, my parents see me that way and, truth be told, I have surpassed my wildest dreams in terms of professional success. But I want to make a difference in the lives of others. I want to be a leader who is known for developing talent no matter their background or ethnicity."

"Wow, congratulations!" I said. "You are building quite a legacy! So how do we get more white men to adopt your mindset?"

"I wish I had the answer to that question. It takes time, of course, and knowledge, but mostly it takes a willingness to step back and look at your life and recognize that we all can make a difference," he responded.

"I wish I could create a pill so everyone could take a stance like yours. May I ask another question? Did you always have this sense of being a leader who could connect across differences, or did you develop it over time?" I asked.

"A little bit of both," he shared. "It was probably always there. But I probably didn't become aware of this passion until I was given my first leadership role."

"So, it takes awareness but also ownership and willingness. I appreciate you for who you are, and I appreciate your support of Lisa," I said.

We moved on to talk about the details of Lisa's growth. When I hung up all I could think about was how to use his story to motivate others. My hope is that you find yourself somewhere in that story.

As a male, you might not understand exactly what women or people of color go through to be accepted, but I bet if you think hard enough you can come up with a time when you felt left out.

Maybe you weren't athletic or you weren't the smartest. I know from having five brothers and being married to Mike for 37 years that men are wired emotionally and feel a lot more than they care to share. And if, by some miracle of God, you don't know what it feels like to be marginalized or treated unequally, but you have children, then you probably know through them because it happens at all stages of our lives.

I think men need to be enlightened.

There are many definitions of the word "enlightened." For purposes of this book, I am defining enlightened as *gaining new knowledge that frees a leader from ignorance about inequalities.*

Can you imagine what it would feel like to know that your children would be subjected to inequities and yet do nothing about it? Absolutely not.

Growth happens at the same pace that you are willing to learn. Building new capabilities to represent the challenges that women and people of color face requires you to do the work. Getting to a space where you can understand what it feels like to be stereotyped, to be the recipient of negative bias or true racism, requires a tremendous amount of empathy. It also requires recognition that you can't continue to approach diversity and inclusion in the same way you did before you were enlightened. You must be willing to create a new level of consciousness.

Einstein said it well with the words, "The significant problems we face cannot be solved at the same level of thinking we were at when we created them."[59] Something in our consciousness must shift for us to be able to see how to act in a way that addresses the challenge of the times.

What beliefs do you have to shift to stand as an ambassador? What must you *unlearn* to make space for new thoughts and a new worldview?

---

59 Albert Einstein, *Only Then Shall We Find Courage* (Emergency Committee of Atomic Scientists, 1946).

THE ELEPHANT IN THE ROOM: WHITE PRIVILEGE

When I started writing this book there was one thing I knew for sure. I knew I would have to deal with the elephant in the room: white privilege.

What is white privilege? Eric Deggans, a journalist, author, pundit and public speaker puts it this way: "Trying to talk about race in America without acknowledging the power of whiteness is like to trying to talk about fire without acknowledging that it burns."[60]

According to *Wikipedia*, "White privilege (or white skin privilege) is a term for societal privileges that benefit people identified as white in Western countries, beyond what is commonly experienced by non-white people under the same social, political or economic circumstances."[61]

So, if you are white in the U.S., you have a 99.9 percent chance that in your life you have been afforded benefits, whether it is qualifying for a house loan, applying for college or shopping at the grocery store. You have been given the benefit of the doubt because of your skin color.

I travel a lot so I observe people's behavior quite a bit. Because I have logged almost three million miles in the air

---

60 Eric Deggans, "It's Called 'Africa.' Of Course It's About Race, Right?" *National Public Radio*, December 16 2013, http://www.npr.org/sections/codeswitch/2013/12/16/251622850/it-s-called-africa-of-course-it-s-about-race-right. Accessed 2 May 2017.

61 Wikipedia contributors, "White Privilege," *Wikipedia, The Free Encyclopedia*, https://en.wikipedia.org/wiki/White_privilege#Definition.

I sometimes get upgraded. A lot of men and women travel these days, but first class is usually predominantly white men. I cannot tell you how many times I have been stopped and reminded that "we are only calling first class," and the white men who are in the same line as I am are never stopped.

This is a small example of white privilege. The attendant assumes that because you are a white male and you are in the first-class line that you must be a first-class ticket holder. But for me, that benefit isn't always extended. There is a question that comes into the heads and hearts of the person doing the assessing as to whether or not a black female really belongs in the first-class cabin, whereas there is an automatic default position taken for white men.

Women and people of color need white men to know that experiences like these undermine and erode confidence and negatively impact engagement. It is an example of micro inequities or *microaggressions* that occur every day.

Microaggression is defined as "brief and commonplace daily verbal, behavioral or environmental indignities, whether intentional or unintentional, that communicate hostile, derogatory or negative racial slights and insults toward people of color."[62]

With regard to gender, some refer to these activities as "mansplaining." Mansplaining is a term that relates to a male communication style of belittlement when explaining something to a female. "Or talking over her, all to explain

---

62 Derald Wing Sue, *Microaggressions in Everyday Life: Race, Gender, and Sexual Orientation* (New Jersey: John Wiley and Sons, 2010).

something she already understands," as Rex Huppke of the *Chicago Tribune* says.[63]

A tremendous amount of energy for women and people of color is spent trying to be accepted rather than trying to add value. Organizations that promote the alpha male style of leadership are not as productive as those cultures that promote a more collaborative style. We will talk about this dynamic in an upcoming chapter.

Recently, I was speaking at a conference about leadership and equality to an audience of more than 5,000 participants, mostly middle-aged white men. I was specifically charged to help this group gain a new appreciation for the power of diversity. My keynote address was followed by a panel discussion, which I moderated. The purpose of the panel was to go deeper into helping the audience understand the steps a leader must take to become a champion for diversity and inclusion.

After the presentations concluded, several participants came to the front of the stage to engage in more dialogue. One gentleman approached me but seemed to back away as others were rushing to engage with the panel members and myself.

"Sir," I said, "do you have a question?"

"No," he said. "I just wanted to say that I appreciate your message, but I think you misunderstand our position.

---

63 Rex Huppke, "The Harm of Mansplaining at Work," *Chicago Tribune* (Chicago, IL), May 13, 2016, http://www.chicagotribune.com/business/careers/ijustworkhere/ct-huppke-work-advice-mansplaining-0515-biz-20160512-column.html.

It's not that I don't care. I do care. I just don't see what you see. I am not a bigot. I am not racist. I have worked hard for what I have received. Yes, I may have some biases, but I am not trying to hurt anyone. I just want to do my work and be a good leader. I don't know that I agree that my success is due to white privilege."

"I get it," I responded. "Maybe you don't see the inequities that are holding women and people of color back. Perhaps it's because you've never thought of the concept of white male privilege. Or maybe you've never seriously asked yourself how you feel about gender equality. The problem isn't just the disparity; it's also those male leaders' *perception* of the issue. Perhaps as you reflect, you will garner a better appreciation for all the subtle ways that white privilege manifests itself."

"If you want to learn," I continued, "you must be willing to challenge the way you see and experience the world — better known as your *worldview*. You must admit that you don't know what you don't know, and you must LISTEN! You can see it if you are looking for it. It may take practice, but I promise you that you will see it. You clearly want to be a good leader or you wouldn't be engaging with me, right?"

"Right, of course I want to become a better leader," he said.

"I respect your desires," I said. "So, because you are aware, you can't go back to the level of consciousness you had before. You are bound to do something about it if you truly want to be a good leader. In the words of Maya Angelou, 'When you know better, you do better.' You now know, and your conscience will hopefully motivate you to do the right thing."

His stare intensified, but he seemed to be at a loss for words.

"Think about your daughters, your sisters, your nieces or your mother," I said. "What about the opportunities they have missed because people like you weren't sensitive to the inequities? You can't speak about something that you know nothing about. You've got to get educated."

"I never thought about it like that," he said.

"Please do think about it," I responded as another participant moved forward to ask me follow-up questions.

As he walked away, I began a familiar conversation in my head I have had with myself many times before. He doesn't get it. He doesn't recognize all the benefits that come along with being a white male. He doesn't know what he doesn't know, I thought. He probably *does* care, but he doesn't know what to do.

Research validates this gentleman's experience. According to the Center for Talent Innovation, "Male CEOs simply don't see the lack of women around them, conditioned as they are by decades of initiatives dedicated to correcting gender inequities."[64]

The first thing men can do to raise their awareness is to simply put up their antennas and pay attention. You

---

64 Sylvia Ann Hewlett, Kerrie Peraino, Laura Sherbin, and Karen Sumburg, "The Sponsor Effect: Breaking Through the Last Glass Ceiling," *The Harvard Business Review Research Report*, December 2010.

can't represent something you don't understand. When we don't understand, we have the potential for engagement in conversations that are loaded with drama, resentment and fear, better known as the "drama triangle." When we are in a place where we feel like we must defend ourselves, we can't learn because we simply are not open.

Those who are in a position to support equality need to understand how white privilege translates into a better position of power and wealth for white men versus non-white male and female colleagues.

"As a group, white guys don't get that American corporate culture — at every level — is the culture of a straight white guy," says Gregg Ward, author of *What Straight, White Guys Don't Get About Diversity & Why*.[65] "Despite this fact, I have found that white men think they get diversity and many of them want to show up as an ally but don't know how. Showing up as an ambassador, champion or ally requires you to understand that there is a double standard. There is no denying that a white man is often escorted by his father or his father's connections to a comfortable seat at the business table. Men must acknowledge that the color of your skin and your heterosexual orientation are the unspoken deciding factors in your success. If you are

65 Gregg Ward, "What Straight, White Guys Don't Get About Diversity & Why," *The Multicultural Advantage*, Accessed May 2, 2017, http://www.multiculturaladvantage.com/recruit/diversity/white-men-diversity/What-Straight-White-Guys-Do-Not-Get-About-Diversity-and-Why.asp.

going to be a part of this work as an ambassador, you must acknowledge that which you may not understand."

The Four Stages of Competence provides a model for learning. This model suggests that people are "unconscious" or initially unaware of how little they know. As they begin to realize their incompetence, they consciously learn a skill then deliberately use it. Eventually, the individual can use the skill without consciously thinking through each step. When this happens, the person is said to have acquired unconscious competence.[66]

Here is the model:

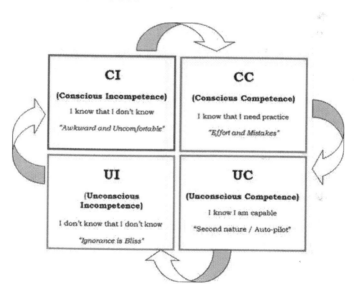

_____

66 Wikipedia contributors, "Four Stages of Competence," *Wikipedia, The Free Encyclopedia*, https://en.wikipedia.org/wiki/Four_stages_of_competence.

White women also experience privilege.

Women connect more easily on women's issues such as pay inequities and advancement opportunities. It becomes decisively harder when the subject of race and privilege comes to the surface. As stated in Chapter 2, women experience defensiveness when it comes to getting to know or support women who are different from them, and white women, especially, fail to recognize or acknowledge difficulties faced by women of color.

If you are experiencing defensiveness as you read this section of the book, I hope that you fight it. This is not about me against you or them against us. This is about opportunity for all of us — men *and* women of all races and identities. It is about stepping into a new level of consciousness that becomes a game changer for you personally, as a human, as a leader and as an agent of change.

So please, don't stop reading. Press on. Let's have the real conversation, and then let's move on. But first we have to have it. White men and women must be willing to see the differences, understand the differences and be willing to take action to mitigate the negative impact that bias, privilege, labels and other more direct forms of racism have in order to serve as early adopters and ambassadors of equality.

I truly wanted to understand why men in particular don't see or understand white privilege, so I asked a dear friend, Greg Magennis, to explain it to me from his perspective. Greg is a white man now living in the U.S., but he grew up in Johannesburg, South Africa during Apartheid.

"Living with my incredible mother, Pauline, who raised my sister, Cara, the eldest and my brother, Sean, the second eldest, and me, I really cemented the idea of manners, respect, honoring elders and being connected to the power and resilience of a strong woman and single mother versus a traditional male-dominated household," Greg shared.

"She was very kind to those who worked with her and always had a team of African painters, gardeners, handymen and cleaners who helped with the houses she was selling or renovating. She was always an entrepreneur on the edge of feast or famine," said Greg. "I remember so vividly the deep respect she had for all people, and she treated them like equals. Not something that was always evident in a world where 'No Blacks' signs barred Africans from using public bathrooms, the beaches, pretty much everything around us, even our schools. Segregation was the order of the day."

Greg continued, "Interestingly, my mum did have difficulty with other white women, particularly with any young girls whom I was remotely interested in. She gave them a very hard time and that saddened me as I felt she was going against everything she taught me when it came to girlfriends and even my wife. She was a staunch Catholic and anything outside the realm of that doctrine was not going to hold any weight for her. I also believe she struggled valiantly with some personal mental challenges that she mostly hid from others, eventually dying from Lou Gehrig's disease at age 78. She also lost three children, going full-term with them, prior to having my sister at age 34. I cannot blame my mum for anything, but she also chose a very tough path for herself which could be vexing to watch."

"My dad was also a great example to us in the way he embraced his staff at his office furniture manufacturing business where everyone loved him across racial lines," Greg added. "The guys I remember well and can recall their names instantly were all either African or what they term 'Coloured' in South Africa, an indigenous race that rose out of European settlers intermarrying with the local African tribes."

"My parents and many of our family made sure to integrate us and connect us children to the most exceptional relationships with those Africans, Indians, Coloureds, Chinese, Portuguese, Dutch and anyone who either worked for them or with them, and it was insisted that we respect and honor who they were as equals. My mum sold to a Chinese family, who owned an incredible Chinese restaurant we used to go to, a house in a 'white suburb' when this had never been done before. She was a rule breaker, and I could tell that she saw others as equal and being entitled to live wherever they wanted to."

"Even with all that," Greg admitted, "I still was vulnerable in my natural prejudice as most people of color were in 'servitude' and kept 'one down' within the society and government of South Africa. There is no question that the social conditioning made me 'feel superior' while always knowing in my gut that I was a bigot and even racist in my thoughts. Fortunately, that mindset never won my heart."

"When I left University, I left my very last 'servant relationship' with an incredible woman, Mavis Stamper, who looked after my house and two boarders that rented from me for my last two years there. Mavis lived in a tiny tin shanty when I first met her, along with three children and a common-law husband. It was crazy," he said.

"By the time I left, I had helped her build a three-bedroom house made of mud-filled walls, without running water but with a faucet in the front of the house where she could get fresh water. There was an outhouse constructed for the latrine. This was like a palace for Mavis, and I gave her my queen-size bed and mattress with linens that I had bought two years earlier. I also gave her as much of my furniture for the kitchen and lounge that she could fit in the house. To this day, I think about her and her family and feel guilty for not being able to still provide employment and help her children with schoolbooks, etcetera. I lost contact with her and wonder if she is still alive and what she is doing and if she is okay."

"I promised myself at age 21," Greg added, "to never have a 'servant' ever again and took on doing all my own housework, washing, ironing, etcetera, to this day. I only use the dry cleaner for my suits. It's like I am performing a penance of sorts, as I can never repay the kindness and love of the 'servants' we had growing up — ending with Mavis who was a gem. I see her smile and beautiful face in my mind's eye and will never forget the privilege that I had and have as a white male in a world that in my lifetime has been completely dominated by white males."

Greg continued, "And then there is a whole story of my military service, two years in the Marine Corps, that also brought to life the deep inequalities and injustices I was privy to. That came before University at age 17. That experience included being court martialed and receiving a severe reprimand on my military record. The commanding officer who charged me was trying to have me locked up in detention barracks for my 'attitude.' I continue to be confronted by white males like this, the latest being our local homeowner's association president here in my city."

"There is a controlling and deeply manipulative and demeaning approach that has been passed down to many white males, and when I see it and experience it I lose any emotional intelligence I may have, and I want to eliminate them deep at my core," he explains.

"If it were not for the incredible love and kindness of Peter Ndluvu, my mum, dad, my siblings and incredible family, I do not think I would have gained the insight that was provided into the realities of life and just how many people, particularly those of minority races, are marginalized and held down by those patriarchs who have been deciding for their own benefit what will and will not be. This brings up so many avenues of thought and experience that confirm my own privilege and bias that I carry with full acknowledgement that I may not even be aware of just how deep my bias actually is."[67]

---

67 Greg Magennis in a discussion with the author, June 2, 2016.

I am so grateful to Greg for having the courage to talk about what no one really wants to talk about: privilege.

He is now a major public champion for equality.

According to Peggy McIntosh in her groundbreaking article, "White Privilege: Unpacking the Invisible Knapsack," she describes white privilege this way: "I think whites are carefully taught not to recognize white privilege, as males are taught not to recognize male privilege. I have come to see white privilege as an invisible package of unearned assets that I can count on cashing in each day, but about which I was 'meant' to remain oblivious. White privilege is like an invisible weightless knapsack of special provisions, maps, passports, codebooks, visas, clothes, tools and blank checks. The pressure to avoid it is great, for in facing it I must give up the myth of meritocracy. The ultimate privilege for heterosexual white men is they do not have to think about or question the dimensions of their identity in the workplace, according to Bill Proudman, CEO of White Men as Full Diversity Partners. If these things are true, this is not such a free country; one's life is not what one makes it; many doors open for certain people through no virtues of their own."[68]

In the work environment, white men are granted the benefit of the doubt that they are great leaders, simply because they are white and men. Research shows that this is one of the driving factors for higher pay increases

---

68 Peggy McIntosh, "White Privilege: Unpacking the Invisible Knapsack," *Peace and Freedom Magazine*, July/August, 1989.

and promotion opportunities. Of course, everyone has to work hard to get to the top, but as Peggy McIntosh points out in her article, white men are handed that "invisible knapsack" full of unearned assets that women and people of color just aren't afforded.

One white female we interviewed, Sheila, who works in human resources, shared a particularly interesting story about how she witnessed white male privilege up close and personal.

She works for a large manufacturing company and oversees several plants. During a talent review, a small group of people, including Sheila herself, were reviewing promotions and associated salary increases. The top two performers in this facility were a woman (Angela) and a man (Paul). Both held the same job during different shifts, though the white male had a few more years of tenure. Sheila shared with the group that it appeared, based upon her analysis, that Angela was being underpaid for doing the same job. The team's immediate response was to take a defensive posture.

Sensing their defensiveness, she told them, "I'm not asking you to defend what has happened, I'm asking you to make sure that we right the wrong that has been done. It is a completely different position."

She told me she was sure that presenting it in this way would click, that the female employee would receive an increase in pay and life would go on. Unfortunately, that's not the way the story goes. She said that one by one, the men in the room (who, by the way, were all white) insisted that Paul receive a high raise as well.

Several of the men sitting at the table chimed in to say that Paul was a family man who had children and needed money to take care of his responsibilities.

Trying to be the voice of reason, she asked about the female employee, didn't she have family responsibilities, too?

"Well, yeah, but she's probably got a husband. She, for sure, doesn't need as much money. I don't know if Paul's wife works. We need to do right by Paul. She will catch up," were the comments of various managers around the room.

She couldn't believe what she was hearing. This wasn't a conversation from 1960; this was a conversation from 2015.

The salary dispute was only resolved by taking the situation to the skip level manager, who determined that the female employee had been underpaid, and it needed to be corrected. But he also granted an increase for Paul that was above the normal increase for performers at his level. When Sheila challenged the skip level manager, she was told, "Paul's a good guy. We need to keep him happy. It will all come out in the wash." Sheila walked away confused and perplexed, wondering how she could get the situation addressed but feeling in her heart she had lost. Some may suggest that in this scenario Paul deserved a higher salary because he had more tenure. But think about it this way — most organizations establish minimum to maximum salary ranges. In most cases the hiring manager gets to decide where to place that employee on the pay grade when the employee is hired. Frequently, men start out at a higher salary range. Paul, more than likely, was hired at a higher salary range than Angela and when their supervisor, Sheila, tried to rectify the situation, the organizational bias became even more overt.

Enlightened male leaders should feel compelled to take action when they observe unequal treatment in the workplace. Why? Because they have invested the time needed to increase their own awareness of their own group, including privileges and disadvantages. They have acknowledged and challenged their own biases and stereotypes and continue to explore the critiques and concepts they most wish to reject.

At the end of the day, they have taken responsibility for their lack of knowledge about women. They are dedicated to building a muscle that allows them to understand and appreciate the journey of others without discounting it. These leaders possess the ability to observe, digest, assess and act when they observe inequities. And they are keenly aware of inequities through education and are willing to use their voices to challenge inequality and drive fairness.

Each of us who are believers in deep democracy must be willing to look and listen with an eye and an ear for justice. There are many people who believe that leveling the playing field to include women and people of color is a zero-sum game. People who believe this are operating from a scarcity mentality.

The term "scarcity mentality" was first coined by Stephen Covey in his bestselling book *The 7 Habits of Highly Effective People*. This mentality materializes as a result of a worldview that makes it difficult to share recognition and power. This worldview robs people of stepping up to serve as ambassadors of this work.

On the flip side, the "abundance mentality" allows leaders to create a paradigm that is rooted in a belief that there are plenty of opportunities for everyone. At the core there is a belief that we can be about winning together. So besides being open, willing and courageous, you have to have an abundance mentality to become an ambassador to drive equality.

What if, in your quest to become an ambassador of equality, you interviewed five people who were from different ethnicities and of the opposite gender as you? And what if you ask them to tell you about their journey in corporate America?

You would hear stories about the invisible barriers that are faced on a daily basis. You would learn how these barriers cause women and people of color to use extra energy as they navigate to be accepted and valued. You would gain a true understanding into whether or not you create environments where these things happen. If you do, then what will you commit to doing about it?

Let me give you a taste of what you might hear.

"It is exhausting," shares Tory in a small group coaching session. "I feel like I have to put on armor every time I go to a meeting. I often feel so alone. No one knows what I go through. In my head, I have to think through every step and every word that comes out of my mouth. If I use a tone that doesn't resonate with others I am perceived as being an 'angry black woman.' If I don't speak, colleagues assume that I have nothing of value to offer. If I speak and challenge someone else, I am a know-it-all and not a team player."

Can you see why it could be so exhausting? You might not know what it feels like to be a woman of color who struggles with these issues, but all of us know what it feels like to be lonely and not feel like anyone around us cares.

As a member of the dominant group, you must be willing to recognize that you don't have to think about being the only one who looks like you in the room. You don't have to think about what you say or even how you say it in most cases. You don't have to wonder if you will be welcomed. If you have a disability, you may identify more easily with the point that is being made. If you are a member of the LGBT community, you feel it.

These variations make it darn hard to show up authentically.

As women and people of color attempt to be valued they lose a piece of themselves. They are constantly *covering*, as we discussed in Chapter 3.

The following examples represent comments made in the workplace, more often than not by members of the dominant group. These can be construed as offensive even if they were not intended to be:

- *"You are so articulate."* Translated by a person of color as, "I can't believe someone from your race is so smart."
- *"You speak English really well."* Translated by an immigrant as, "You are not from my culture. You're an outsider."
- *"I have several friends who are from your culture."* Translated by the person of color as, "I am not racist. See? I have friends of color."
- *"Everyone can succeed in the U.S. if they just work hard enough."* Translated by women and people of color as, "You need to work harder."
- *"You should be happy with a successful rating considering where you come from."* Translated by women and people of color as, "I do not believe you are capable of more than a mediocre performance."

Those in leadership roles need to keep a watchful eye out for statements such as these, as they send the signal that "you are not a part of the dominant group." As you deepen your understanding of the challenges faced by women and multiethnic groups, the natural next step occurs as you continue to learn, and that is to teach others.

My hope is that you get excited about sharing what you have learned with others. There are literally hundreds of teachable moments that ambassadors can tap into every day. Teachable moments arise as you ask questions and are created when one person is willing to share a perspective that enlightens another. They happen when you spend your time and energy serving as a coach and mentor to others.

To achieve these goals, we all need to relax in our learning about differences, because you won't be perfect. There is a certain amount of uneasiness that comes with this territory. Work through it by challenging your assumptions. In fact, assume nothing.

Ask more questions; make fewer statements.

Most of the time people are not aware that what they have just said or done is offensive. The intent was not to belittle or undervalue someone else, but the impact *did* belittle and the behavior *does* send signals that one is not valued at the same level as the dominant group.

This next message is for those men who are open and want to become a leader who remains relevant. For you, I want to start by asking a question: "What don't you know about diversity and inclusion that would allow you to move from *awareness* to *advocacy* to *adaptation*?"

I would humbly submit that getting started requires a willingness to ask questions and engage in conversations. Demonstrating a willingness to acknowledge, listen and understand the gender and race inequalities facing women and people of color is a huge step in the right direction. It's an unwillingness to engage in conversation over the issues that perpetuates the problem.

Honest conversations stimulate reflection, and sometimes one conversation can be so convicting that it creates a paradigm shift to enlightenment.

My hope is that you become convicted to think differently about justice, fairness and equal opportunities. I also hope this reflection stirs an authentic desire in you to step out as an early adopter and model the behavior that others should follow in the creation of leadership behaviors and cultures that support deep democracy.

COURAGEOUS CALL-TO-ACTION REFLECTION QUESTIONS

- How can your behavior demonstrate that you respect the human dignity of every person that you meet?
- What challenges do you see that the dominant group (white men) creates for women and people of color in the business world?
- Are you courageous enough to call out inequities when you observe them happening? Can you offer an example of when you have done this or perhaps when you should have done this?
- Are you open to embracing the perspectives of others without defending your own perspective, particularly if they don't align with your own?
- Are you guilty of mansplaining, a.k.a. speaking over women and even other men when you want to drive a point home? How can you become more aware of this habit?
- Do you speak to women or people of color in ways that send the signal that you are discounting their comments and contributions to a conversation? If so, how can you alter this language?
- What have you learned about diversity that would stimulate the creation of a very deep and personal connection to equality? How will you go about developing and building new capabilities that enable you to truly connect across differences?

Five

The Courage to Get Messy

"The world is changed by your example,
not by your opinion."

-Paulo Coelho

Anyone who is familiar with my leadership development programs knows that I preach the importance
of showing up as a thought leader with significant sub-
stance, savviness and style. I often referred to this combi-
nation as being "buttoned up."

So, as we begin this chapter, I am going to do a 180
and tell you that in order to make progress in driving
equality we are going to need to get "messy." That's right,
messy. Perhaps you, like me, have wonderful memories
of getting messy as teenagers. I can remember playing
touch football in the rain and loving it. Unfortunately, as
we grow up things become so serious, and we are taught
to be "appropriate" in our behavior.

But appropriate behavior when talking about race and gender requires a high level of vulnerability and a willingness to get uncomfortable. In other words, a willingness to get messy.

Recently, I was leading a session where a conversation about race was taking place. I was moderating the conversation in a room of 250 women and a few men. I stopped at a table to check in on the conversation and what I heard absolutely convinced me that this notion of being messy is spot on.

"I don't know what to call you people," a white female said to an African-American female that she had been partnered with to complete a table exercise. "I mean, I feel like I don't know what to say and that doesn't make we want to have the conversation."

The African-American female was gentle in her response, "I want you to see me as a woman and as a black woman," she said.

"Yeah, but what do I *call* you?" the white female persisted.

"Call me by my name," the African-American woman said.

"But, really. Do you want to be called black, African-American or what?" said the white female.

I could see the African-American female starting to get tense so I inserted myself and shared with both of them that it was okay not to know what to say, it was okay not to know how to say it but to just to be open, curious, interested and authentically willing to challenge your assumptions. That's the only way the conversation is going to get to a place of true connection, I shared. I told them they didn't have to know anything to start the conversation about race and gender. They just had to be willing to explore.

After our quick discussion, I stepped back from the conversation so that they could begin to re-engage each other. I could see the tension on both of their faces start to disappear. What happened?

The white female gave up trying to put everything into a little box that could be managed. The African-American female, in my opinion, saw a woman across from her who really wanted to learn. But they both had to be willing to step in a path of unknown. In this "unknown" space we can create new connections across differences.

At another table, a white male and an Asian female were engaging in the discussion of race and the workplace. As I approached, I heard him say, "I don't want to lower the standards so that people who aren't excellent are given the job over someone that I know would do a great job."

"Tell me more," I said. "Who are these people you believe are below standard?"

He became clearly disturbed as I probed. "You know," he said.

"No, I don't know," I responded.

"Well, Hispanics, blacks, you know...people who are not as good as white people."

"What makes you feel like these people would not be as good as or better than a white person?" I continued.

"I don't know," he responded. "I just feel that way."

"So, you prefer to hire white people because you believe that they represent the best, is that right?" I asked.

"Well..." he stumbled.

"It's okay," I said. "You are telling your truth. I don't think that it is right, but it is your truth. You are biased. You believe because of your life experiences that white people, primarily white men, are the best employees. I applaud you for speaking your truth."

You could see the others at the table showing expressions that suggested that they were not comfortable with me giving him an out. I wasn't giving him an out. I was making space to get messy. You see, until we talk about our truths, we can't influence anyone. We have to let people speak their truth. In return, we can start a dialogue. If we shut people down then we get nowhere. Getting messy requires us to be uncomfortable and to try and understand why people feel the way that they do. Then we can ask the powerful questions that help to illuminate the bias and engage in a different kind of conversation.

In a diversity and inclusion boot camp that I have designed to help people have these types of messy conversations, we do an exercise that is quite telling. The exercise involves the placement of flip charts around the room with descriptors such as: white male, white female, black male, black female, Asian male, Asian female, Hispanic male, Hispanic female, gay male, gay female and the list continues. The intent is to list as many cohorts that work within the organization. We even have a chart for single women, single parents and so forth.

Then the participants are asked to take sticky notes and place positive or negative stereotypes that they believe society holds for each group. I have done this exercise more than 100 times. And every time, the descriptors for white men state that they are smart, leaders, powerful, capable and responsible. Asian men are often labeled as smart, but they don't get any of the other positive attributes that are associated with white men. They get descriptors like quiet, aloof, and hard to get to know. In fact, no other group gets the type of positive descriptors that are used for white men. Black men are viewed as lazy, athletic, baby daddies. Black women receive descriptors such as angry, baby mommas, loud. White women fair a little better than all the other women, but they, too, receive more negative descriptors than white men. They are viewed as unreliable due to having babies, looking for Mr. Right to take care of them, etc.

So, is it any wonder that the gentleman who shared his thoughts about believing that white men were the best would be any different? Here's the deal. The question is asked in a way that gives the participants an out because this is what *society* thinks.

At the end of the day, corporate America is a reflection of society.

This, my friend, is why more progress is not being made in the advancement of women and people of color. Men and women see white men as the best leaders.

Despite the efforts of diversity and inclusion programs, we are not getting to the core issues of our beliefs about differences.

In fact, according to a *Harvard Business Review* article entitled "Diversity Policies Rarely Make Companies Fairer, and They Feel Threatening to White Men"[69] authors Tessa L. Dover, Cheryl R. Kaiser and Brenda Major share the outcomes of a longitudinal study of over 700 U.S. companies. The research, according to the authors, found that implementing diversity training programs has little positive effect and may even decrease representation of black women.

Most people assume that diversity policies make companies fairer for women and minorities, though the data suggests otherwise. Even when there is clear evidence of discrimination at a company, the presence of a diversity policy leads people to discount claims of unfair treatment.

In previous research, we've found that this is especially true for members of dominant groups and those who tend to believe that the system is generally fair. So as long as we don't acknowledge the unfairness, the inequities, the bias that laden cultures throughout the United States of America, we will continue to make only painfully slow progress.

---

69 Tessa L. Dover, Brenda Major, and Cheryl R. Kaiser, "Diversity Policies Rarely Make Companies Fairer, and They Feel Threatening to White Men," *Harvard Business Review*, January 4, 2016.

In the same article mentioned above, research from a different experience indicated that groups that typically occupy positions of power may feel alienated and vulnerable when their company claims to value diversity. This may be one explanation for the lackluster success of most diversity management attempts: When people feel threatened, they may resist efforts to make the workplace more inclusive.

There are schools of thought that suggest the way to drive equality is to remove the bias out of processes. I agree that mitigating biases from organizational process is critical to the success of equality. Having said that, however, I don't believe that getting people to acknowledge their biases nor removing bias from the system will help us to realize the changes that are needed to create work environments where everyone has equal opportunity. I think that it takes courageous conversations that awaken a level of human consciousness. This awakening allows us to get beyond the titles and skin color, beyond the perceptions, beyond the bias and into a human-to-human connection.

In the research for this book, we surveyed 30,000 men and women across different industries to gain a better understanding of why more progress isn't being made to create equality. Our findings validate the need to move beyond political correctness and get real about the truth beliefs that leaders hold about fairness, about connecting across differences and about taking action to drive equality.

We asked respondents this question: What holds you back from stepping up and stepping out as a champion for diversity and inclusion and equality?

The #1 response was, "It's not on my radar screen." Followed by, "I don't know how to get started." No wonder the dominant group believes that everything is okay and that the business world is fair. They are not living the experience that members of the non-dominant group is living.

And it's not just white men, it's white women, too. White women are much more easily received by white men. White men have a context for white women. In other words, they can conjure up an image of a white woman who has played a positive role in their lives as a sister, mother or grandmother. It is much harder for white men to do that for multicultural women. As a result, we have underdeveloped relationships. White women, based upon our research, are far more comfortable with other white women. So they, too, shy away from building authentic relationships with multicultural women.

Perhaps as you read this you find yourself saying, "That's me."

And that's okay.

If that is your starting point, start there. I challenge you to understand that every one of us is diverse. This includes white men. And I invite you to realize that we all have biases.

In a 2014 Deloitte report covering key human resource trends, diversity and inclusion was consistently reported as one of the least important issues on leaders' minds compared to other HR matters.[70] What's more, a SHRM report confirmed that among the Fortune 1000, a full one-fifth of respondents indicated their organizations have very informal diversity efforts with nothing structured at all, with 41 percent of study respondents specifying the underlying reason being that they're "too busy."[71] If D&I is to be a real business imperative, equality has to become a priority on everyone's radar screens, and we must stop making excuses. We must learn.

I use an assessment in my diversity and inclusion immersion learning programs called IDI. IDI stands for the Intercultural Development Inventory.[72] It is based upon a model created by a professor named Milton Bennett. That model was then refined by Mitch Hammer who ultimately created the assessment. This assessment helps people understand their starting point on connecting across differences. The IDI is a statistically reliable, cross-culturally valid measure of intercultural competence. The inventory

70 Deloitte, *Global Human Capital Trends 2014*, https://dupress.deloitte.com/dup-us-en/focus/human-capital-trends/2014.html?icid=hp:ft:01.

71 Society of Human Resource Managers (SHRM), *SHRM Survey Findings: Diversity and Inclusion*, April 8, 2014. https://www.shrm.org/hr-today/trends-and-forecasting/research-and-surveys/pages/diversity-inclusion.aspx.

72 Mitchell R. Hammer, Milton J. Bennett, Richard Wiseman, "Measuring Intercultural Sensitivity: The Intercultural Development Inventory," *International Journal of Intercultural Relations* 27, no. 4 (2003).

generates a graphic profile of an individual's or group's predominant stage of development in intercultural skill. Knowledge of an individual or group's predominant orientation toward culture difference serves as the foundation for developing meaningful behavioral change management strategies.

Intercultural Development Continuum

Monocultural Mindset

Adaptation

Acceptance

Minimization

Polarization

Intercultural Mindset

Denial

The Developmental Model of Intercultural Sensitivity (DMIS)

This model helps us understand how we relate across differences.

If you are in the Denial stage, you mainly relate to those who are similar to you. This is what is referred to as *Ethnocentrism*. On the flip side, when you are able to relate across all kinds of differences, your orientation is more toward Acceptance and Adaptation. This is referred to as *Ethnorelativism*.

Let me offer a brief recap of this powerful tool:

Denial: A Denial mindset reflects a more limited capability for understanding and appropriately responding to cultural differences in values, beliefs, perceptions, emotional responses and behaviors. Denial consists of a Disinterest in Other Cultures and a more active Avoidance of Cultural Difference.

Polarization: Polarization is an evaluative mindset that views cultural differences from an "us versus them" perspective. Polarization can take the form of Defense ("My cultural practices are superior to other cultural practices") or Reversal ("Other cultures are better than mine"). Within Defense, cultural differences are often seen as divisive and threatening to one's own "way of doing things." Reversal is a mindset that values and may idealize other cultural practices while denigrating one's own culture group.

Minimization: Minimization is a transitional mindset between the more Monocultural orientations of Denial and Polarization and the more Intercultural/ Global worldviews of Acceptance and Adaptation. Minimization highlights commonalities in both human Similarity (basic needs) and Universalism (universal values and principles) that can mask a deeper understanding of cultural differences. Minimization can take one of two forms: (a) the highlighting of commonalities due to limited cultural self-understanding, which is more commonly experienced by dominant group members within a cultural community; or (b) the highlighting of commonalities as a strategy for navigating the values and practices largely determined by the dominant culture group, which is more often experienced by non-dominant group members within a larger cultural community.

Acceptance: Acceptance and Adaptation are Intercultural/Global mindsets. With an Acceptance orientation, individuals recognize and appreciate patterns of cultural difference and commonality in their own and other cultures. An Acceptance orientation is curious to learn how a cultural pattern of behavior makes sense within different cultural communities. This involves contrastive self-reflection between one's own culturally learned perceptions and behaviors and the perceptions and practices of different cultural groups. While curious, individuals with an Acceptance mindset are not fully able to appropriately adapt to cultural difference.

Adaptation: An Adaptation orientation consists of both Cognitive Frame-Shifting (shifting one's cultural perspective) and Behavioral Code-Shifting (changing behavior in authentic and culturally appropriate ways). Adaptation enables deep cultural bridging across diverse communities using an increased repertoire of cultural frameworks and practices in navigating cultural commonalities and differences. An Adaptation mindset sees adaptation in performance (behavior). While people with an Adaptation mindset typically focus on learning adaptive strategies, problems can arise when people with Adaptation mindsets express little tolerance toward people who engage diversity from other developmental orientations. This can result in people with Adaptive capabilities being marginalized in their workplace. When an Adaptation mindset is present in the workplace, diversity feels "valued and involved."

Cultural Disengagement: Cultural Disengagement is not an orientation on the Intercultural Development Continuum. It involves the degree of connection or disconnection an individual or group experiences toward a primary cultural community.[73]

This is a basic recap of the model. If you are serious about building cultural competencies that will allow you to truly drive equality, taking this assessment would be a great starting place. I use it to get conversations started about differences. And courageous conversations are occurring across the country and, in some cases, the world.

Just the other day I was reading *The Broadstreet Review*[74] and noticed something that was really interesting. By the way, *The Broadstreet Review* is a daily

---

73 Mitchell R. Hammer in conjunction with Intercultural Development Inventory, LLC, "The Intercultural Development Continuum," *Intercultural Development v. 3(IDI),* 2012. https://idiinventory.com/products/the-intercultural-development-continuum-idc/.
74 http://www.broadstreetreview.com/.

newsletter that offers the reader a recap of the major activities impacting women across the world. It is offered by *Fortune*. If you aren't subscribed to receive it, I highly recommend it. Their short articles give the reader a thought-provoking jolt. And the snippet that caught my attention speaks to the recent flurry of activity within organizations to get their employees to acknowledge their biases.

This particular article that caught my attention was offered by *Fortune* Associate Editor Valentina Zarya. And it went something like this...

I FAILED THIS TEST ON RACISM AND SEXISM — AND SO WILL YOU

It's a Thursday afternoon and I'm in a room full of people I just met, admitting things to them that I have yet to fully admit to myself. I am biased against all minority groups, I tell them: women, African Americans and homosexuals. My confession doesn't incite anger or shock. On the contrary, the audience nods with empathy. They tell me it's to be expected—they have biases, too.

This may sound like group therapy or a meeting of Bigots Anonymous, but it's actually an increasingly popular tool in corporations across the U.S.: unconscious bias training. Organizations including Facebook, Coca-Cola, Google and the CIA have all embraced such sessions, which aim to increase employees' awareness of their own prejudice and teach them how to guard against it.

Like me, most Americans tend to be biased in favor of the white, male, heterosexual majority—even when they themselves do not fall into that group, according to find-ings by Project Implicit, a Harvard University-run nonprofit focused on studying social cognition.

Employers are now under immense pressure from investors, employees, and even the White House to miti-gate these biases, which studies have shown can nega-tively affect a company's bottom line. In the last couple of years, a growing number of companies have taken steps to air their diversity dirty laundry by releasing annual reports about the makeup of their workforces.

She failed and so will you and so will I.

But once we take the step of peeling back the first layer of the onion, then what? Then we have to have the *real* conversation or all that happens is that employees go around acknowledging biases but never really developing a true appreciation for how those biases impact the lives of other people.

A good friend who began as a client put it like this, "I had to first realize that I had biases. Second, I had to be willing to gain a true understanding of the journey of women who don't look like me. As a white female, I have not had to think about the challenge of dealing with gen-der AND race. As I began to engage in the real conversa-tions (the messy ones), I truly realized that I don't know enough about the journey of women of color to serve as an advocate. I have a seat at the table, but I don't know how to use the power of the seat. I'm willing to learn but without the *real* conversation I don't believe that white women and women of color can form a collective voice.

And we definitely can't speak truth to the dominant group who is in power. We don't know what we don't know."

The conversations don't have to feel like a two-by-four hit you. Rather, if done right, it's a path to growth for everyone involved. But here's the point: The conversation will change your perspective. Once your eyes are opened, you must make a choice to develop thoughts that will shape your habits and behaviors. But it all starts with the acquisition of the new knowledge.

"'In my mind, I see a line. And over that line, I see green fields and lovely flowers and beautiful white women with their arms stretched out to me over that line. But I just can't seem to get there — no-how. I can't seem to get over that line.' That was Harriett Tubman's view in the 1800s," said Viola Davis after receiving the Award for Outstanding Lead Actress in a Drama at the 2015 Emmys. She went on to say that "the only thing that stood between black women and more success was opportunity."[75]

"The truth is this," said one white female executive, "white women don't understand enough about the journey of women of color to represent them at the table. I think that we want to, but we just don't know how. We don't know how to challenge. We are afraid. We are not confident and, as a result, we are silent. I hate to think that

---

75 Viola Davis, "Viola Davis Gives Powerful Speech About Diversity and Opportunity at Emmys 2015," 2015, YouTube video, 2:42. Posted September 2015. https://www.youtube.com/watch?v=OSpQfvd_zkE.

I have become the very version of someone I don't want to be. I want to be able to support great talent — period."

"Yet fear reminds me of the costs I would pay in the organization where I currently work for speaking against the establishment's thinking," she continues. "I had a recent experience that really caused me to pause. I was sitting in an executive talent debriefing where a president of a business unit expressed his frustration about not having women on his team. His excuse was that he would promote women to other organizations in an attempt to help the company."

"Right," she thought to herself at the time. "The truth is that you are hiding behind your own beliefs that women are not capable of running a sales organization. Yet I didn't say anything. I just didn't. I had this whole conversation in my head about what I wanted to say, but the words just didn't come out of my mouth."

Without the willingness to step out in traffic and get messy, voices will continue to be silenced. Whatever we give our attention to gets bigger. In this case, she gave attention to fear and it grew to the point that she couldn't show up as her authentic self.

We have to choose confidence over fear.

Sounds easy, right? Wouldn't it be great if it were easy? So what's the problem?

The problems (plural) present themselves when we reject each other's truths. We discount people's stories. "Oh, it can't be that bad…" or "Aren't you taking this a little too personally?" or, better yet, "That can't be true."

Let me give you an example…

I was teaching a session on inclusion several years ago. One of the modules focused on white privilege. There were about 30 people in the class, 90 percent of whom were white. It was a mixture of men and women. One of the African-American men shared a story with the group about an experience that he had in his neighborhood. He talked about being pulled over by a neighborhood police officer as he entered the gated community where he lived. Clearly he had access into the property, as it was a gated community.

"Why are you stopping me? What's the problem?" he said to the patrol officer.

"I want to know what you are doing in this neighborhood," said the patrol officer.

"I live here," said the African-American male.

The exchange continued and eventually the African-American male was encouraged to go home. The African-American male told the group that the only reason why this happened was because he was black.

The white men and women immediately begin to defend the actions of the patrol officer at the expense of challenging the truth of the story. They didn't know the patrol officer. They knew their colleague, but nonetheless they didn't embrace his story. They felt compelled to defend the police officer. I chimed in and shared the numerous times that my husband has been stopped in neighborhoods where we've lived by city police for no reason. Again they discounted, saying things like, "Well, there could be many reasons for your husband being pulled over."

When we discount each other's stories, walls go up. I could literally give you hundreds of examples where I have personally observed this dynamic. The #1 rule to the success of a courageous, messy conversation is this: Accept the other person's truth as truth. Period!

Here's a truth that we all need to accept…

The experience that each of us has in the business world is directly connected to our gender and race. And for people of color, more often than not, our experience is not as good as our white male and female counterparts.

What's the evidence? Countless studies including research we conducted for this book. The numbers outlined in the first chapter also validate that women of color — indeed, *people* of color — are at a competitive disadvantage for obtaining opportunities in the business world because we are not members of the dominant white group.

"Women HAVE to serve as a community of supporters for each other,"[76] Indra Nooyi stated at the Inaugural Wal-Mart Global Women's Forum.

I agree.

While there are many definitions that could be associated with the word "community," for the purposes of this

---

76 Indra Nooyi, interview by Judith McKenna, *Performance with Purpose*, Walmart Women's Forum 2015. http://corporate.walmart.com/global-womens-forum#.

book, I am defining it as *a feeling of fellowship with each other, not a feeling of competition*. Even more specifically, this community is made up of women and men that will use their voices to advocate for equality. Whether that is in the succession planning session where the majority of the decision makers are white or it is in policy discussions about work-life flexibility or it is talking about a product that the organization is making to serve the female population.

We all need to become feminist.

A lot of people hear the word feminism and have an immediate negative response. That is until they learn that *the definition of a feminist is a person who believes in equality.*

It's that plain and simple.

Let's stop being afraid to have the real conversation about race, bias and equality. Let's touch our truth. Let's get messy, stop labeling and learn to support each other across differences so that we can create a business world where everyone is afforded equal opportunities to experience success and contribute at their highest levels.

It is the right thing to do for so many reasons, including better business results. All of this requires that you make a choice. The choice is to challenge your current thinking and beliefs and acquire new experiences with those who are different from you so that you build new beliefs about those who are not just like you.

I AM NOT BLACK, YOU ARE NOT WHITE.
By Prince Ea

I am not Black
I mean, that's what the world calls me, but it's not...me
I didn't come out of my mother's womb saying, "Hey everybody, I'm...Black."
No, I was taught to be black
And you were taught to call me that
Along with whatever you call yourself
It's just a...label

See, from birth the world force feeds us these...labels
And eventually we all swallow them
We digest and accept the labels, never ever doubting them
But there's one problem:
Labels are not you and labels are not me
Labels are just ...labels
But who we truly are is not... skin... deep
See, when I drive my car, no one would ever confuse the car for.... me
Well, when I drive my ....body, why do you confuse me for my... body?
It's....my....body....get it? Not me

Let me break it down
See, our bodies are just cars that we operate and drive around
The dealership we'll call society decided to label mine the "black edition,"
Yours the "Irish" or "White edition"
And with no money down, 0% APR, and no test drive
We were forced to own these cars for the rest of our lives
Forgive me, but I fail to see the logic or pride
In defining myself or judging another by the cars we drive
Because who we truly are is found inside

Listen, I'm not here to tell you how science has concluded that genetically we're all mixed
And race in the human species doesn't exist
Or how every historian knows that race was invented in the 15th century
To divide people from each other and it has worked perfectly...
No.... I'm not here to lecture
I just want to ask one question

Who would you be if the world never gave you a label?
Never gave you a box to check?
Would you be White? Black? Mexican?
Asian? Native American? Middle Eastern? Indian?
No. We would be one; we would be together
No longer living in the error
Of calling human beings Black people or White people
These labels that will forever blind us from seeing a person for who they are

Equality

But instead seeing them through the judgmental, prejudicial, artificial filters of who we THINK they are

And when you let an artificial label define yourself
Then, my friend, you have chosen smallness over greatness and minimized your.... self
Confined and divided your .....self from others
And it is an undeniable fact that
When there is division, there will be conflict
And conflict starts wars
Therefore every war has started over labels
It's always us... versus them
So, the answer to war, racism, sexism, and every other -ism
Is so simple that every politician has missed it
It's the labels...
We must rip them off

Isn't it funny how no baby is born racist
Yet, every baby cries when they hear the cries of another
No matter the gender, culture or color
Proving that deep down, we were meant to connect and care for each other
That is our mission, and that is not my opinion
That is the truth in a world that has sold us fiction
Please listen, labels only distort our vision
Which is why half of those watching this will dismiss it
Or feel resistance and conflicted

But, just remember...
So, did the caterpillar
Before it broke through its shell and became the magnificent butterfly
Well, these labels are our shells and we must do the same thing
So we can finally spread our wings
Human beings were not meant to be slapped with labels like groceries at supermarkets
DNA cannot be regulated by the FDA
We were meant to be free
And only until you remove them all
And stop living and thinking so small
Will we be free to see ourselves and each other for who we....TRULY.... are[77]

---

77 Richard Williams, "I Am NOT Black, You Are NOT White," YouTube video, 4:35. Posted November 2, 2015. https://www.you-tube.com/watch?v=q0qD2K2RWkc&feature=youtu.be.

COURAGEOUS CALL-TO-ACTION REFLECTION QUESTIONS:

- How does your current position on the continuum impact your ability to connect across differences?
- Why is moving along the continuum important to you?
- What steps are you willing to take in order to move along the continuum and expand your cultural competencies?

Six

Courageous Conversations About Forging Meaningful Partnerships Across Differences

"If you want to go fast, go alone. If you
want to go far, go with others."

—AFRICAN PROVERB

At a Fortune 1000 company a few years ago, I was conducting a two-day workshop on diversity and inclusion. An older white gentleman named Frank came up afterward and told me that our topics and discussions had really resonated with him.

"My daughter and I have had a really difficult time the last several years," he shared. "And those difficulties were directly connected to race. You see, she fell in love with a black man and had a baby with him. My father was still alive and would have nothing to do with the baby. I am ashamed to say that the first time I actually met the baby was when he was already a toddler."

I was riveted, and he continued, "It was in that moment I realized that love has nothing to do with race. I realized that I could no longer allow myself to live in the past; to think the things I was taught to think about people who were not white. At that moment, when I looked at that child and realized he was my blood, something happened to me. The power of love overshadowed the old stories. Where we're going now is that I will love this baby, claim this baby. I will not let old thoughts rob me of a relationship with my child and a relationship with my grandchild."

I loved hearing Frank's story. He learned something we all must learn — he *owned* his story. He knew it wasn't about his past; it was about where he was going. And he learned the power of sharing his story.

Coming from a white man, that is absolutely invaluable.

When I think about my life and the people who have helped me, I can say with a tremendous amount of conviction that white men have played a dominant role in the success I have experienced. In fact, I have been helped professionally by more white men than any other demographic or gender. As I shared in Chapter 2, I have not had positive experiences gaining support from women of color and *definitely* not from white women until very recently.

So here is what I believe about the role that white men currently play regarding driving equality:

There are just not enough believers.

Those who DO believe are true champions, but they are not the majority.

Since 2009, I, like others, have been talking about the importance of getting men on board, primarily white men given that they are the dominant leaders in corporate America. We were really talking about this before 2009, but no one was listening.

It wasn't that long ago when people were offended when you used words like "white men," "dominant group" or "majority group." Using this kind of language made both men and women uncomfortable. While it was obvious, no one wanted to talk about the role of white men in advancing a world of equality.

I was recently part of a research team whose aim was to gain a better understanding of what men and women in the business world thought about the role of diversity and inclusion. In a survey sponsored by the Network of Executive Women, we reached out to 8,300 Network members and 15,776 NEW supporters. The survey was completed by 1,950 recipients, a response rate of 8%. Ninety-six percent of the respondents were women and 4% were men. Nine senior executives were interviewed by phone and email. When asked, "How important is diversity and inclusion to your company's performance?" Seventy-one percent said that diversity and inclusion is very important. What is notable about that number is this: The majority of men and women recognize the immense importance of diversity and inclusion.

We also asked, "Do you think white men have an advantage in hiring and promotions in the consumer products and retail industry?" Fifty-nine percent said yes, acknowledging that white men have an advantage. Even white men recognize this fact.[78]

So, what's the problem?

Here's the deal: It's been said several times already that we all have biases — every one of us. It is up to us to engage in the courageous conversations to help us rid ourselves of the biases that cause us to not connect across differences.

Each and every one of us must reflect on this. And men, I am asking you to spend some extra time in reflection. Some extra time thinking: Who is in your inner circle? Who do you default to for promotions? Who do you hang out with at the bar? What do you know about the journey of women or people of color in the business world?

I challenge you to get out of your bubble. We need for you to do what you say you do best — LEAD!

In one of our most recent surveys, we focused on the intersection of race and gender, and a few interesting polarities came to the surface. When we asked respondents, "Do women of color face greater bias than white women?" the results were intriguing. Forty-two percent of non-Hispanic white respondents agreed with this

---

78 Network of Executive Women Consumer Products/Retail, *Tapestry: Leveraging the Rich Diversity of Women in Retail and Consumer Goods*, 2014.
http://workforceexcellence.com/wp-content/uploads/2015/06/Tapestry_Leveraging_Women.pdf.

statement, while 80% of minority respondents — almost double — agreed.

However, when we asked respondents, "Do white women have an advantage in the workplace?" only 13% of non-Hispanic white respondents agreed, compared to 63% of minority respondents agreeing.

This data suggests that real disparities of perception exist between race and gender. We can infer that gender and race have both their advantages and disadvantages in the workplace. Additionally, there appears to be a hierarchy of the advantages and disadvantages, where white men have the ultimate advantage and women of color have the ultimate disadvantage.

A BIZARRE STATE OF DISCONNECT

I recently interviewed a black female who is a principal for a large consulting group and specializes in neuroscience. In fact, she earned a Ph.D. in neuroscience. I met her at a diversity event sponsored by her company, and we struck up a conversation.

Appointment as a principal is no easy task to achieve, and I was both inspired by and thrilled for her success. I could tell she was really smart, but I had no idea at that point that she had Ph.D. in neuroscience, from MIT no less. We enjoyed the conversation and promised to keep in touch.

As a follow-up, I reached out to her and scheduled time to chat again. During that conversation, I probed to understand her journey to success. I asked what challenges she had faced in building a career within her organization. Her answer was not surprising.

"Credibility," she said.

"But," I said, "you have a Ph.D. in a really challenging area — the brain."

I knew exactly what was going on, but I wanted her to tell me her story, so I continued to probe. She told me of a recent experience she shared with a white male colleague that explained her point of view.

She told me that she and this colleague were both trained in neuroscience, and they were both attending — get this — an unconscious bias training class. During the exercises, other colleagues continued to tell them how much they had in common and encouraged the two of them to connect. She was excited and introduced herself to him.

"He would not look me in the eye," she said.

I asked her why she thought he was engaging in this manner.

"He didn't want to view me as his equal," she responded. "He wasn't comfortable with the fact that a black female was as educated as he was. It is a blessing and curse being smart. He didn't respect my competence. His default was simply that, 'She can't be that good.' I have seen him give white male colleagues immediate respect and credibility, but unfortunately that is not the treatment I got. I wish people could see beyond my skin color and just recognize and value my contributions. His unconscious behaviors send the signal that he doesn't respect me or my talents. Who would want to work for a company where your colleagues don't respect you?"

"I appreciate your point of view," I shared. "I remember when I was in corporate myself. I was the only female in a group of 20 leaders. All of my colleagues were white men. One of the things that happened quite frequently was very similar to your story. I would introduce an idea and no one would respond. It was as if they weren't listening. Then not five minutes later, one of my colleagues would reframe my same idea and the entire team thought that it was the best thing to happen since sliced bread. It was so incredibly frustrating."

I wish I had known the science behind that behavior like I do now. Research shows that men respond to the tone of another man over a woman. And men often dominate the conversation or meeting.

Victoria L. Brescoll, a Yale psychologist, studied legislators and found that male senators with more power, as measured by tenure, leadership, and other measurable data, spent more time on the Senate floor than their junior colleagues. Female senators, on the other hand were not afforded more speaking time on the floor no matter how much power they had. [79]

79 Sheryl Sandberg, Adam Grant, "Speaking While Female," *The New York Times* (New York, NY), January 12, 2015. https://www.nytimes.com/2015/01/11/opinion/sunday/speaking-while-female.html?_r=0.

Professor Brescoll suspected that powerful women often stay silent for fear of repercussions, so she took her research to the corporate sector. She asked professional women and men to assess the competence of executives who voiced their opinions more or less frequently. And you know what she found? Male executives who expressed their opinions more often than their associates were rewarded with 10% higher ratings of competence. Female executives who spoke out more than their peers were punished, both by men and women, with 14% lower ratings. As this and other research proves, women who worry about talking "too much" because it may cause problems for them are not just being paranoid. They do have something to worry about. "This speaking-up double bind harms organizations by depriving them of valuable ideas."[80]

Not even Supreme Court justices are immune from what some are calling "manterruptions," meaning a man interrupting a woman while she's trying to speak. Researchers at Northwestern University have found that as more women join the Supreme Court, more instances of male justices and male lawyers interrupting the female justices have occurred.[81] According to the study's author, Tonja Jacobi, "Interruptions are often regarded as an

---

80 Ibid.
81 Claire Zillman, "Ruth Bader Ginsburg Used This Simple Trick to Cut Down on 'Manterrupting'," *Fortune Magazine*, April 2017. http://fortune.com/2017/04/06/ruth-bader-ginsburg-supreme-court-advice-interrupting/.

assertion of power through verbal dominance." Women often use polite phrasing like "excuse me," "may I ask" or "pardon me" before asking a question or making a comment in a meeting. The study's authors suggest that women eliminate such phrases. In fact, Ruth Bader Ginsburg has done just that. She has ceased being so polite and has started using a more aggressive style of questioning. It must be working because she is being interrupted less and less frequently.[82]

One of my coaching clients, a white female, was promoted to a director position. She reported to a VP, a white male. I was called in to ensure that she made a successful transition from the manager to the director role. Almost immediately the male VP's biases negatively impacted the relationship. As it turns out, he was a strong left-brain individual, and she was skewed more toward the right brain. For those of you who have been exposed to the implications of these two different styles, you can see how this story is going to unfold. She was known for her people strengths. She was viewed as collaborative, results-focused and a great communicator. He was viewed as a thinker, slow to make decisions and extremely analytical.

No matter what information she submitted to him, it would be returned with several red markings with questions like, "Where are the facts?" even though the facts were clearly there. In his mind, the information hadn't been presented in the way that he wanted to see it.

---

82 Ibid.

Despite being able to influence her colleagues to raise their overall performance, nothing she did was ever good enough for him.

For a year she battled to build a relationship with this man. Unfortunately, he never came around to being open to her style of leadership. It was his way or no way. The impact of this experience robbed her of her confidence and her belief that she could reach her ultimate goal of obtaining a Senior Vice President position within the organization.

Here's the big kicker. He got promoted despite his inability to connect across differences of thinking and working styles. She was demoted, unfortunately, and is now in the process of rebuilding her professional reputation.

This is a classic example of the experience that women have with men who haven't acquired cultural competencies.

MEN: YOU ARE A PART OF THE EQUATION

I also think that men don't know what they don't know. Many of them don't see themselves as a part of the diversity and inclusion movement. Well, here's the first thing that I need to tell you: White men are diverse. Truth be told, unless you were born as a full-blood Native American, you are multicultural as well.

I remember during one of my keynote addresses on women and men coming together to advance the full embodiment of diversity and inclusion, I was engaging the audience and asked three white men, "Where are you from?"

Each of them looked at me in total bewilderment as to why I was asking the question. Each of them cautiously responded, "I'm from America."

"What is your heritage?" I persisted. Each of them again responded with "American."

"Ok," I said, "let me ask you the question a different way. Where were your grandparents or great-grandparents from?" It was then that it clicked. They, like most of us, came to America from other parts of the world. One man then said his background was Irish. Another one chimed in and said that his folks were German.

"And so," I said, "do you see that you, too, are multicultural?"

It was clear that they hadn't thought about it that way, and it was clear that it made them very uncomfortable. We should all celebrate the fact that we represent a blended, multicultural nation. This is why they call America "the melting pot."

Yet there are those who think that we need one culture in the United States of America. There are leaders who don't believe in the benefit of a multicultural nation, let alone an inclusive multicultural company. We heard such statements throughout the highly polarized 2016 Presidential campaign.

When we look a little further into the backstory of these kinds of statements, we find that there is a school of thought that diversity is "white genocide." And soundbites like this one: "We are losing our culture and way of life." Translated differently? White men are losing their power, and they don't like it.

I have personally experienced white men and women making statements like, "You've had a black President. What else do you guys want?" This is an example that speaks to an underlying issue — fear of loss. The truth is that the demographic shifts happening in America are not going to stop. Leaders who recognize the trends and pro-actively develop the skills to interact with a changed work-force and marketplace will win. Those who do not, won't.

"I can't get help from any of the men, as a multicultural female," one executive shared with me. "White men are afraid of me, Asian men don't know me, black men don't want to be seen with me, and men from other cultures of the world are confused by me. What can I do?"

This is just one statement of the frustration that women of color expressed during our research. No wonder compa-nies are struggling with such high turnover among this group.

"I feel like men discount me. I want to experience suc-cess just like them."

The research backs up her statement. Roughly equal numbers of men and women say they want to be pro-moted, 78% and 75%, respectively, according to *The Wall Street Journal.*[83]

What does all of this tell me?

---

83 Nikki Waller, Joann S. Lublin, "What's Holding Women Back in the Workplace?" *The Wall Street Journal* (New York, NY), September 30, 2015. https://www.wsj.com/articles/whats-holding-women-back-in-the-workplace-1443600242.

That men who don't see the true and powerful benefits of diversity and inclusion just don't get it. It is more comfortable for us to talk about gender differences than get to the courageous conversations about ethnicity. It brings up stuff from the past that people want to ensure remains in the past. But because we have never had the courageous conversations, feelings of resentment, fear, isolation and rejection continue to come up and will continue to until the point where we really touch the truth.

EVOLVING THE MALE STYLE OF LEADERSHIP

In the groundbreaking book *The Innovator's Dilemma: When New Technologies Cause Great Firms to Fail*, Clay Christensen introduced a notion of disruption and business sustainability. He closely examines the role that technology plays in transforming businesses and industries. He suggests that when companies fail it is because management failed to pay attention to the trend or fought the trend.

There is another trend that many leaders ignore, and that trend is this: Women and multicultural women will shape their company's future, at least in North America.

Consider these facts:

- Companies need to become more collaborative if they are going to increase their speed to market.
- Companies need to become more inclusive if they are going to be able to attract top talent.
- Companies are going to need to shift from rewarding leaders who behave in a command-and-control

model to one that is more of mentor/coach if they are to raise employee engagement.

So how do these facts link to women, and why should *you* care?

Women are more collaborative, inclusive and intuitive, according to research. When it comes to leadership in the workplace, work teams made up of mostly women tend to share leadership roles more than teams dominated by men, says a University of Toronto organizational behavior expert.

"Women tend to prefer egalitarian norms in work groups whereas men favour hierarchical structures," says Jennifer Berdahl, business professor at University of Toronto's Rotman School of Management and lead author of the study published in the March issue of *Group Dynamics: Theory, Research and Practice*. This, in turn, influences how men and women work together on teams, she adds.[84]

The business world needs us. So why aren't more men carrying the female flag given their knowledge about these trends?

Because of bias, arrogance and pride.

What is interesting, though, is that younger men are more supportive of women than older men. Younger men

---

84 Jennifer Berdahl, Cameron Anderson, "Women More Collaborative in Workteams," *Group Dynamics: Theory, Research and Practice*, March 2005.

acknowledge the importance of equality. They recognize that corporate America must change, but they just don't have the power yet to do anything about it. According to Deloitte's Millennial Survey, most Millennials believe the corporate sector is having a positive effect on society and the world's economy. However, they do think corporations can do more to tackle social challenges like "resource scarcity, climate change, and income inequality." [85]

Millennials are often seen as trendsetters and "predictors of the next big thing."[86] A Nielsen.com article states that "Today's Millennials are the most racially diverse generation in U.S. history, with nearly 43% identifying as non-white."[87] The article goes on to comment on their spending power. "Varying estimates place this group's purchasing power anywhere between $125 billion and $890 billion annually while some estimates attribute these young shoppers with $200 billion of direct buying power plus an additional $500 billion in indirect influence, based on Millennials' powers of persuasion over their Baby Boomer parents."[88]

---

85 Ray Williams, "How the Millennial Generation Will Change the Workplace," Psychology Today (blog), March 19, 2014, https://www.psychologytoday.com/blog/wired-success/201403/how-the-millennial-generation-will-change-the-workplace.

86 "The Men, the Myths, the Legends: Why Millennial 'Dudes' Might Be More Receptive to Marketing than We Thought," Nielsen.com, December 10, 2014, http://www.nielsen.com/us/en/insights/news/2014/the-men-the-myths-the-legends-why-millennial-dudes-might-be-more-receptive-to-marketing.html.

87 Ibid.

88 Ibid.

The movie industry is even starting to take notice of the gender pay gap. Folks really sat up and took notice when actress Jennifer Lawrence published a "provocative blog piece about the disparity in wages for women in Hollywood. Her friend and frequent co-star Bradley Cooper took a bold stance to talk about pay equity and committed to changing the status quo."[89]

Like Lawrence and Cooper, the Millennial generation is not going to tolerate the corporate behavior that has been passed off as status quo for the last 20 years. They are passionate about inequities and will be bringing them to light whenever they see them. This is terrific news for your company, if your company is ready.[90]

In my second book, *The Hybrid Leader*, I wrote about the importance of valuing traditionally "female" labeled traits. Men and women lead differently. That's no new revelation. What *is* new for organizations is to recognize the attributes of the female style of leadership. And what's even more important is for both men and women to recognize that they both have strengths that would be characterized as strengths of the other gender.

How can this be? Because each of us was born with a left side and a right side of the brain.

What has been rewarded for decades are characteristics traditionally associated with the left side of the brain.

89 Jeffery Tobias Halter, "The Four Core Values of Millennial Women," http://www.newonline.org/news/259642/The-4-core-values-of-Millennial-women.htm.
90 Ibid.

Leaders who were known for their visionary and strategic thinking skills were praised, while leaders who were more collaborative and intuitive were viewed as weak.

In today's quick-paced, ever-changing market, collaboration, innovation and intuition have taken on greater levels of importance. These are right-brain functions.

So, what's the secret to leading in today's world? A big part of the answer lies in the ability to tap into both sides of the brain. To achieve this goal, we are all going to have to challenge our belief systems and learn some new things.

As an example, when boys are little and they stub their toes, they are told to suck it up. They are encouraged to be a big boy and are told that big boys don't cry. Then they grow up and enter the working world, and we ask them to show some emotional intelligence. It is no surprise that they are at a loss when asked to do something they have learned not to do because of cultural expectations and limitations.

On the flip side of the coin, when little girls stub their toes, they are told to cry it out. And when they come into the business world and show emotion, they are told that they have their "hair on fire" and are too emotional.

The business world needs leaders who can bring a balanced skill set and perspective. I call this style of leadership a *hybrid* because it represents the best of male and female leadership styles. It is a new style of leadership.

Honestly, it is time to redefine leadership. It is one of the best steps to take to eradicate bias. And it is exactly what is needed to manage a diverse workforce as well as a changing and more demanding consumer and global economy.

Today's leaders must be able to coach, mentor and inspire their employees. In order to do this, they must be able to connect with them as humans and, as humans, we are wired emotionally. Think about what happens to grown men when they walk their daughters down the aisle at their weddings, or their team loses the Super Bowl, and they hide their faces in their hands. They cry. They feel emotion. They connect.

I think most leaders recognize the need for a new style of leadership. I just don't think that, up until now, we have had the courageous conversations about the strengths of men and women. And I definitely don't think the business world has created an expectation that leaders must be collaborative. In fact, the compensation systems aren't even set up in a way that rewards collaboration, but that's a topic for another book.

A different style of leader is needed because it is this different style of leadership that will be open to supporting women and people of color. It is a true leader who can make the head and the heart connection. And you know what? Leaders who move to a more balanced style of leadership are better people managers, better strategists, better agents of change and better business leaders. These leaders get that leadership is personal. It is about your life's experience and using it in a way that creates equality.

The fact is that men who have become champions for equality usually become champions because of a personal cultural experience.

Such is the case with one of the male executives I interviewed. I simply asked why he believed in diversity and inclusion.

He shared, "It is personal to me because I have children. My intellectual connection is the reasoning behind why I support diversity and inclusion and my company's commitment to the cause. My family and my faith are what promote me to be visible about advancing diversity and inclusion."

He continued, "I would say that even if I didn't have the faith, I would be convinced intellectually because of the numbers. Ten years ago, when I was asked to be the diversity champion for the department I was working in, I knew we had a problem. We were not promoting women and people of color at the same rate as white males, Asian males and Israeli males."

"I really observed that it was true that people promote people who look like them. It makes them comfortable. I started realizing that this was a human dynamic," he stated. "The second thing I noticed was that my diverse teams were outperforming those that were not diverse. I got curious. I started reading about it. I looked at why the United States had done so well in the world. My eyes opened up to see and appreciate that the diversity of America was a *benefit* for us. It challenged me to ensure that I was building a diverse team that would be a high-performing team. It was later on that the personal connection came into it."

"You see, my daughter turned out to have an inclination for science and math. She was doing group projects at school, and the boys in her groups would take over the projects. In fact, the teacher separated the girls from the boys in one of her engineering classes. This incident really impacted her confidence. I told her she should apply to Stanford. She was so hesitant to apply because of her experiences. I really had to encourage her and stretch her to do it. She was totally surprised when she was accepted. In reality, she should have realized that she was smart and deserved to be included."

He concluded, "The data needs to be shown more often. Leaders need to be held accountable for their area of responsibility — including their people. It can't be a once-a-quarter event. The advancement of women and people of color should be visited as a challenge to the business. If we can appeal to the reasoning of an individual, that is the first thing. I think the second thing is to convince them of the value of diverse teams. You need to be able to prove that diverse teams perform better. Finally, I think that men need to have experiences that allow them to *feel* what non-dominant group members experience when being left out. Let them compare that to what it feels like when they are invited to be a part of the dialogue and are included."

GETTING TO THE 17%

"So how do we get other men to feel it, believe it, and own it?" I asked him.

"Find the 17% and go from there," he stated simply. "Research relating to innovation says that dramatic change starts in a small group of innovators. Right now there are too many leaders who are saying the right thing because they know they have to comply. We need to get people convicted to take action and behave differently. Find the men that are predisposed because of their upbringing or life experiences."

So, what's up with the 17%?

In Christensen's book mentioned earlier in this chapter, he references the need to get 17% on board first to believe in a new idea, technology, strategy or change. Then, he says, once you get that group to buy in, you can create momentum and the momentum starts with obtaining 17% of the target group's buy-in.

There have been several thought leaders who have referenced this model including the Rogers' Adoption model. In this model, there are 2.5% of folks who are the innovators. These are the people who have the courage to try something, knowing that there is a possibility of failure. They are so determined that they push forward. As a result, they influence the next critical segment of the population referred to as the early adopters.

The early adopters make the innovators look extremely thoughtful, creative and wise. The early adopters are the 13.5% who are willing to demonstrate new behaviors that support the innovators' concepts. Early adopters are like early champions who serve as ambassadors to influence the next group of followers — the early majority of followers. The remaining two groups are late adopters and laggards.

There are a number of CEOs who have established themselves as innovators. We've spoken about Don Knauss and James White and we'll speak about Muhtar Kent shortly. I think it's fair to say that a majority of the C-suite could be placed in an early adopter position, although I would say that their commitment has a lot more to do with their financial compensation than it does with creating a legacy. I realize that this is a general statement, but this is what I have observed based upon working in this space for 15 years.

So now I am asking you — a man — directly, are you a male who will publicly declare your commitment to driving equality in the workplace? Do you want to be known as an early adopter?

We need to get to the tipping point where a minimum of 17% of all men in the business world believe in the importance of equality in the workplace and in society. Then we will be able to create serious momentum.

A lot of people would say that men, particularly white men, are currently thriving in the work environment. I don't agree. I see a group of white men who are in powerful positions (most of them Baby Boomers) who grew up in a society where the role of women has been evolving. But that role is still a bit fuzzy in their minds. Most of these men had mothers who stayed at home to raise them while their fathers pursued the professional path. Intellectually they recognize that the workplace is changing, but they haven't found the emotional connection. And they think that the pain is not quite real because they don't experience it personally.

Then there is a growing population of men who are actually struggling with how to "show up" in the business world. There is so much pressure to adopt the behaviors of the preferred style of leadership that, like women, men find themselves assimilating. This is why, in my opinion, we haven't been able to build the early adopters who truly want the workplace to change to a place of equality.

As I mentioned earlier, men in different generations think much differently about what they want in a corporate experience and also how they see equality. I recently conducted a strategic planning session for a Fortune 100 company. There were 16 people in the room, almost a 50/50 split of men and women. The majority of the participants were white, with the exception of two Asian men and two women of color. Two of the participants were clearly from the Millennial generation.

The conversation covered the employee lifecycle, including recruiting, onboarding, development and advancement. This company, like most out there, was experiencing a struggle with retention and advancement of women and people of color. As the dialogue continued, it became apparent that one of the two Millennials was a gay white male.

As he shared his experience with the company, he used language that the group didn't expect.

"I want to be treated equally," he shared. "I don't want to have to fight the 'good ol' boy' clubs. I am a white male, but the biases against gay men are very obvious in this company. So, I understand why women and people of color are struggling because I feel it, too."

There was a moment of silence.

My response to this situation was simply that it was clear that there was a need for courageous conversations about the experiences of employees from a number of diverse groups within their company. And I thanked him for starting one of those conversations.

So how do we get to the 17%? How do we create a majority who believe in the power of women and people of color as true leaders? These are the questions we need to solve in order to make transformational progress.

We need each other. Does it matter who reaches out first? No. Both men and women need to reach across the aisle and gain new insights and then build a new collaborative approach to creating a workplace where everyone can win. That's what true partnerships do: create a place where *everyone* can win.

I believe that partnerships move beyond advocacy. They actually move into creator positions. To do this, we have to stop talking *at* each other and take a true stance of curiosity with a commitment to building something new *with* each other.

AN IRRESISTIBLE PROPOSITION

White men believe they are already winning. And for the most part, they are. But the landscape is changing. There is such a dramatic shift occurring that if white men (and *all* men, for that matter) don't get on board, their future success and the future success of their children is at risk.

With leaders who get it, there is a sense of urgency for men and women to become allies in driving equality, a feeling that we don't have one minute to lose. This assumes, of course, that you *want* to win. Women will shape the global economy over the next decade.

Muhtar Kent, CEO of The Coca-Cola Company, shared in a *Huffington Post* article[91] an enlightened moment that caused him to rethink the future of business. As CEO, he is clearly responsible for the key areas of focus (the strategic imperatives) that must be addressed in order for Coca-Cola to succeed. In the article, he tells the story of driving to work in Atlanta, getting stuck in traffic and turning the radio station to NPR. Listening to NPR was a part of his daily routine.

That day on NPR, the commentators were discussing China and its role in shaping future success globally. After reflecting, he shared this, "It isn't going to be China, nor the BRIC countries that will shape the future. Instead it will be women!" This enlightened moment caused him to

---

91 Muhtar Kent, "This Century Goes to the Women," *Huffington Post*,
http://www.huffingtonpost.com/muhtar-kent/post_1057_b_762044.html

take several serious steps towards achieving full representation of women in his company, starting with his board.

So, what is the irresistible proposition?

The proposition is about your success. If you want to continue to thrive in the business world, you need to get enlightened yourself. Even more important, the enlightenment needs to spark deep conviction for you to become an early adopter.

Let me put it as straight as possible: The innovation has begun. It began a long time ago, but now it is time for early adopters to step up. The innovators, early adopters and majority leaders who sign up for advancing equality in the workplace will be the winners. The rest? Not winners.

EARLY ADOPTER BEHAVIOR

I would like to ask you to evaluate yourself on a scale of 1 to 10 using the following behaviors that my research and the research of others associate with early adopters of equality. Early adopters:

1. Embrace equality intellectually and emotionally. They make it personal.
2. See equality as a means to add more value to the customer/consumer.
3. Ask women for their opinions and value the response.
4. Don't discount experiences shared by others who are different as irrelevant or not true.
5. Actively listen and are curious.

6. Know how to leverage "collaboration" across differences to create new opportunities.

7. Innovate. They refuse to get into a state of contentment. Rather, they are dissatisfied with the status quo.

8. Are willing to take risks.

9. Are willing to stand alone in boldness to drive new patterns relating to the business, people and organization.

10. Are willing to challenge their own biases (conscious or unconscious) and admit that they don't know what they don't know.

11. Are willing to engage in messy conversations about race and gender equality.

12. Challenge women to represent themselves as "ready now" because you know there is a default position women take that reveals they want to be 100% ready before they embrace a promotion opportunity.

Let me leave this chapter with an example of what an early adopter partnership looks like in real life: *Morning Joe* co-hosts Joe Scarborough and Mika Brzezinski.

It was actually Joe who mentored Mika to understand, first, that she was being underpaid and, second, how to negotiate to get fair pay. He made it personal. He didn't have to do it, but he did because he believes that equal pay is what everyone deserves. He knew it in his head and felt it in his heart. This is what it takes for any of us to want to take action. We have to know it and believe in it. We have to be stirred to a point where we must talk about the inequities that we see.

Indeed, all of the courageous trailblazers who put themselves out in the midst of people who did not believe in their work were stirred. They felt convicted. They were relentless. They did not back down, and they intentionally told anyone who would listen in an effort to build partnerships they believed would help their cause.

I was really moved by a PBS *Frontline* interview with Dr. Bennet Omalu. You may recognize the name from the movie *Concussion*, starring Will Smith. A forensic pathologist, Omalu conducted the autopsy of Pittsburgh Steelers' former center Mike Webster, which led to the discovery of a new disease that he named Chronic Traumatic Encephalopathy (CTE). He is currently the chief medical examiner of San Joaquin County, California, and a professor in the UC Davis Department of Medical Pathology and Laboratory Medicine.

He was moved to do what was right because it was right. He demonstrated such courage in taking on the NFL. In the interview, he shared that he honestly thought that the NFL would be grateful for his discovery. Sadly, they weren't. Why? Well, the obvious. It represented change. It represented a complete shift in the beloved game that is America's game.

The thing is, Omalu knew also that to advance his findings, he would need allies. Partners. He reached out to other physicians. He collaborated in the development of a white paper. He reached out to former players. He submitted his paper to reviewers.

I don't want to give away too much more in case you do decide to watch this very powerful movie, but I do want to say this: Nothing that ever comes into reality happens because of one person. It happens because one person is willing to build partnerships and support. And they create a groundswell.

It is time for a groundswell.

COURAGEOUS CALL-TO-ACTION REFLECTION QUESTIONS

- Men, how aware are you of the challenges that women face in building a successful career, including equal pay?
- Women, what have you done to connect across generations and ethnicity?
- Women, are you equipped to represent *all* women, including those not of your own ethnicity?
- Leaders, are you intentionally serving as sponsors across gender and ethnicity? Is building partners who support equality a part of your leadership agenda and platform? How and in what specific ways?
- How would you respond if your children asked you the question, "Do you believe in equality in the workplace?"
- Do you believe that all people bring something good to the table?
- Do you believe that white people experience privilege?
- Have you prepared yourself to have the needed courageous conversations to engage men in the support of advancing women in your organization?

Seven

Courageous Conversations About a New Style of Leadership

"Fight for the things that you care about.
But do it in a way that will lead others to
join you."

—SUPREME COURT JUSTICE RUTH BADER GINSBURG

What is clear to me and hopefully now clear to you after the last chapter is a simple but profound truth: We need a new style of leadership.

"Men have a unique opportunity in this as we still make up 80% of the executive ranks and even more than that at the CEO level," said Julio A. Portalatin, Mercer President and CEO. "We have a unique obligation to be out in front on growing women in the workforce. It's not a 'women's' issue. This is a workforce issue."[92]

I would take it a step further and say that driving equality for women and people of color is a business sustainability issue. To get to the heart of this conversation, we must admit that the current style of leadership has been designed by men for men.

In 2006, I wrote my second leadership book, entitled *The Hybrid Leader: Blending the Best of the Male and Female Leadership Styles*. Since then, there have been countless articles and special reports advocating for the creation of a leadership style that reflects both genders.

THE FEMALE STYLE OF LEADERSHIP

Organizations are finally beginning to recognize the need for a shift by adding such expectations as agility, collaboration, inclusion and coaching into their leadership expectations. By the way, these are traits that are primarily associated with the female style of leadership.

Yes, women do lead differently. We have different approaches to decision-making and different communication styles. Women are more empathic. This doesn't

---

92 Julio A. Portalatin, "The Role of Men: Leading the Charge Together," (presentation, World Economic Forum Annual Meeting, Davos, Switzerland, January 20, 2016).

mean that men have outdated skills. It simply means that we need to create a style of leadership that draws on the strengths of both genders.

To do this, we must embrace three things:

1. It is time for a new style of leadership.
2. Women bring a lot (but not all) of what is needed to form the new style.
3. Men and women have to develop new capabilities that neither currently has.

Most of the skills that women bring to the table are thought of as "soft skills."

It is worth spending just a few minutes making sure we understand the journey of women in the workplace. The increase of women in the workplace actually began in the early 1900s. World War I created a need for women to work as men left for war. Their contributions were significant. They demonstrated solid leadership, resilience and the ability to rally not just the people they were responsible for but to keep the community strong. Once the men returned from the war, however, women were displaced. This time period was followed by the feminist movement, which fought to minimize the differences between men and women. While this movement had good intentions, it caused women to try to act like men. I know that some will disagree with this statement, but it is my personal opinion, so take it for what it's worth.

"I love being a woman and I was not one of these women who rose through professional life by wearing men's clothes or looking masculine. I loved wearing bright colors and being who I am."[93] Former U.S. Secretary of State Madeleine Albright was ahead of her time. How many of you remember the days when women, myself included, wore those hideous blue suits with the giant shoulder pads better suited for football players? I will be the first to admit that when I was in the corporate world, I totally tried to act like a man. I could curse as well as the guys and could pop a Budweiser at 7 a.m. on the golf course. In fact, I could knock back two by 8:30 a.m. I knew I was in trouble when I started scratching my thighs. I was trying to act like a man, and it was absolutely, positively ridiculous!

Women are not having the same experience in the business world as men. And women of color have it even worse.

"You won't find many women or multicultural women candidates considered for senior jobs, because their leadership style is different. For instance, Asian women tend to be hardworking but fairly soft-spoken when it comes to their style. This is rarely acceptable as a leadership style,

---

93 Madeleine Albright, Quote. https://www.brainyquote.com/quotes/quotes/m/madeleinea433594.html.

even if that woman has delivered great results with that style,"[94] shares Joy Chen, CEO at H20+Beauty.

I couldn't agree more with Joy. Organizations say they want diversity of thought and even go as far as saying they want diversity of leadership style. In reality, however, everyone is held to a model of leadership that was created *by* white men *for* white men.

What is that model? It is the John Wayne "I can solve any problem myself" model. I have an answer to every question. I'm not responsible for motivating employees. Rather, I'm responsible for firing those who can't motivate themselves.

"They call them the 42-long leaders," said Tonie Leatherberry. "That means the men who are recognized as 'leaders' are usually 6'2", blond hair, blue eyes, former athletes who are all-knowing."[95]

My intention in sharing this is not to put down white male leaders. I really want to get everyone to recognize how our limited perceptions of what leaders look like and act like are wrong.

So, what should this new style of leadership look like?

I think it begins with acknowledging that it is time to reset what has been known as "traditional" competencies. I am not suggesting that we toss out the current

---

94 Joy Chen, interview by Network of Executive Women Researchers, *Tapestry: Leveraging the Rich Diversity of Women in Retail and Consumer Goods*, 2014.

95 Tonie Leatherberry, discussion with the author, January 5, 2012.

leadership competencies. And no, there is no one-size-fits-all leadership model.

But what's really important in a leader's style in today's world? According to PEW research, honesty, intelligence and decisiveness are considered "absolutely essential" leadership qualities by at least eight in 10 adults based upon their survey. A closer look at this survey reveals that these qualities are followed by two traits that are associated with women. Sixty-seven percent of those surveyed in the time period of November 18-21, 2014, said compassion followed by innovation are critical qualities leaders need in order to be effective.

Men and women tended to agree on the importance of the top-tier leadership traits. Women are much more likely than men to say that being compassionate is absolutely essential in a leader. And 61% of women place a higher value on innovation than men do. Finally, women are more likely than men to say ambition is an essential trait for a leader (57% women compared to 48% men say that this is absolutely essential).[96]

I would suggest that there is another trait that needs to be included as a critical leadership trait. That is *cultural competency*. Think about it. We say that diversity, inclusion and gender equities are critical to the success of the business, yet we don't expect any of our leaders to be

---

96 Pew Research Center, *Women and Leadership: What Makes a Good Leader, and Does Gender Matter?* 2015. http://www.pew socialtrends.org/2015/01/14/chapter-2-what-makes-a-good-leader-and-does-gender-matter/.

able to demonstrate the very trait that is connected to this so-called "business imperative."

To help develop cultural competency, organizations must move from hierarchical, top-down leadership models to a *partnership leadership style*.

These partnership leaders value *people* as the greatest asset of the organization. They are rooted in a belief that every single person, no matter their background or gender, brings value to the table. They believe in nurturing and developing this talent. They know that coaching and mentoring is the best method to unleash potential. This style of leadership is committed to obtaining results but equally committed to ensuring that employees are treated fairly. This style is focused on the "who" and the "how." Leaders from the traditional model of leadership are primarily focused on the "how" and often leave dead bodies along the way.

Have you ever been in a brainstorming meeting and observed one idea after another being discounted? This, in spite of the fact that the meeting began with a call from the host leader to "value diversity of thought"? We can't value each other's thoughts if we don't value different perspectives. It's like there are unwritten rules that say if you haven't been invited to speak, then you can't speak. These unwritten rules are formed by the "in" group, and everyone else is on the outside.

A few weeks ago, I moderated what my client calls a "listening circle." It is a brilliant way to tap into the brainpower of your customers and potential partners. The focus of this particular session dealt with getting more females into the typically male-dominated fields of science, technology, engineering and math.

The audience was all women, and it included a young member of Generation Z. Generation Z is the generation after Millennials, and they have completely different expectations of how they will be treated in the business world. This Generation Z female was a lovely actress and philanthropist — those were the words that she used to describe herself in the introduction. Well, she didn't use the "lovely" part; I took the liberty of adding that word.

She was 16 years old. Only 16! She asserted herself and made some really useful and insightful comments at the start of the meeting. We then came to a point in the discussion where we were talking about using a digital platform. Most of the women there were Generation Y or Baby Boomers, and we were all talking over ourselves. I could see that she wanted to again join in the conversation, so I called her name and asked her to chime in.

She proceeded to give us a bit of insight on the role that social media plays in creating a relationship with girls her age. It was brilliant. Who knew that a little word called "liked" (in reference to Facebook accolades) could be so powerful! Go figure.

We all celebrated the power of the diversity of thought and paused to give her public acknowledgement of her contributions. She felt good, and we felt good. How hard was it? It wasn't. It just required intentionality.

You can do this too! Leaders who believe in leveraging diversity of thought make space for the contributions of others. They are aware of how cultural sensitivities may impact a woman's level of engagement. They invite participation by making it safe to be wrong, safe to come across not as astute as others and even safe to mispronounce words because English might not be their first language.

Empathy is linked to building your cultural competency skillset and is the ability to experience and relate to the thoughts, emotions or experience of others. Research from the Center for Creative Leadership (CCL) has shown that the nature of leadership is shifting, placing a greater emphasis on building and maintaining relationships.

Leaders today need to be more people-focused and able to work with those not just in the next cubicle but also with those in other buildings or other countries. Past CCL research such as the Changing Nature of Leadership shows that leaders now need to lead people, collaborate with others, be able to cross organizational and cultural boundaries and create shared direction, alignment and commitment between social groups with varying histories, perspectives, values and cultures.[97]

It stands to reason that empathy would go a long way toward meeting these people-oriented managerial and leadership requirements. Having empathy is not the same

---

97 Andre Martin, "The Changing Nature of Leadership," *A CCL Research White Paper*, 2007.
http://www.ccl.org/wp-content/uploads/2015/04/NatureLeadership.pdf.

thing as *demonstrating* empathy.[98] Conveying empathic emotion is defined as the ability to understand what others are feeling,[99] the ability to actively share emotions with others and passively experiencing the feelings of others[100] in order to be effective.[101] Fortunately, empathy is not a fixed trait. It can be learned.[102]

In 2014, Simon Sinek wrote a bestselling book about leadership entitled *Leaders Eat Last: Why Some Teams Pull Together and Others Don't.* Another must read if you haven't read it already. I have read literally hundreds of books on leadership and have written two books myself. I was profoundly moved by the idea that Simon puts forth in this book. He argues that leadership has very little to do with title, authority, business acumen or being in charge. Instead, Sinek says that leadership is about empowering others to achieve things they didn't think were possible.

I am totally biased here as I wholeheartedly believe in his words regarding leaders being willing to place others'

---

98 Changming Duan, "Being empathic: The role of motivation to empathize and the nature of target emotions," *Motivation and Emotion* 24, no. 1, 2000.

99 Changming Duan, Clara E. Hill, "The Current State of Empathy Research," *Journal of Counseling Psychology* 43, no. 3 (1996).

100 Daniel Goleman, *Working with Emotional Intelligence.* (New York: Bantam Dell, 2000).

101 Janet B. Kellett, Ronald H. Humphrey, Randall G. Sleeth, "Empathy and the Emergence of Task and Relations Leaders," *Leadership Quarterly* 17, 2006.

102 Johanna Shapiro, "How do physicians teach empathy in the primary care setting?" *Academic Medicine* 77, 4, 2002.

needs above their own. In my book *The Hybrid Leader,* I proposed that the best leaders are vested as equally in their people's success as in their own.

Sinek was moved by an experience he had in the Marine Corps. He observed how, at chow time, the most junior ranks ate first. Others followed until the highest-ranking officers ate last. What he found interesting was this: There was no rule that the lower levels *had* to eat first. It was just the way the higher-ups viewed their responsibilities as leaders.

My future son-in-law, Ryan Brence, is a captain in the Army, and I spoke with him about the way the Army approaches leadership. I wanted to know more about what promoted a mindset of being responsible for another colleague's life.

Many of you might remember that in 2015, history was made regarding females in the military. According to CNN, Captain Kristen Griest and 1st Lt. Shaye Haver were the first two women to graduate from the U.S. Army's elite Ranger School. They graduated in Ranger Class 08-15 at Fort Benning, Georgia, after completing weeks of grueling physical training across woods, mountains and swamplands. Sadly, there were many who argued that the standards had been reduced so that women could become Rangers. Defense Secretary Ash Carter vehemently argued differently, saying that these two women were trailblazers. Some of their male classmates said the two women at various points in the course were the only ones to volunteer to take on the heavy weight of their male counterparts.[103]

Ryan shared that when you become a Ranger, you are assigned to serve as a buddy to another Ranger. If the Ranger who you are assigned to falls asleep at their post, guess what? The buddy is called out and reprimanded — not the Ranger who fell asleep.

I was really taken aback, because I agreed that's how it should be in the business world. We should be looking out for each other. We should care about each other's aspirations. We must be aware. We must listen, and we must be willing to learn.

Well, I am certainly no Ranger, but I agree that it is time to stop making excuses for why more progress hasn't been made to create equality. Leaders (both men and women) must respect the power of inclusion and the need to close the gap.

LEADING AS A CHAMPION FOR EQUALITY

A leader cannot demonstrate empathy without a certain level of curiosity and a willingness to be vulnerable. Fundamental to leading with a focus on empathy is trustworthiness. In her new book *Presence*, Harvard Business

---

103 Ray Sanchez, Laura Smith-Spark, "Two Women Make Army Ranger History," *CNN*, updated August 21, 2015. http://www.cnn.com/2015/08/21/us/women-army-ranger-graduation/index.html.

School Professor Amy Cuddy says people quickly consider two questions when they first meet you:

Can I trust this person?

Can I respect this person?

Psychologists refer to these dimensions as warmth and competence, respectively, and ideally you want to be perceived as having both. Interestingly, Cuddy says that most people, especially in a professional context, believe that competence is the more important factor. After all, they want to prove that they are smart and talented enough to handle your business.[104]

But in fact, warmth and trustworthiness as well as active listening and caring are important factors in building authentic relationships and making authentic connections.

Going back to the 1940 Ohio University study on leadership, trust, respect, warmth and empathy were called out as critical to the role of leadership. Research studies have asserted for some time that emotional intelligence is the true source of leadership success and impact. Unfortunately, the leadership capabilities that are rewarded in today's business cultures place more importance on competence. But the fact of the matter is that we

---

104 Jenna Goudreau, "A Harvard Psychologist Says People Judge You Based on 2 Criteria When They First Meet You," *Business Insider Australia*, 2016.
http://www.businessinsider.com.au/harvard-psychologist-amy-cuddy-how-people-judge-you-2016-1?r=US&IR=T.

work with humans, and humans are wired emotionally for connection and community.

Steven P. Brown, a futurist who is a white male, puts it this way: Leaders must respect that the other person probably knows something you don't know.[105] The assumption must be that they have something that could help you. In fact, it could be something that might even save your butt. Brown suggests that we are in the "collaboration economy." The only way that companies will win is to drive higher levels of collaboration and connecting with people who are different in all kinds of ways. He suggests, based upon his experience, that collaboration is the key to innovating and remaining relevant. He shared a story that makes this point.

More than a decade ago, he observed the power of a team trusting each other, valuing different ways of thinking and collaboration. He shared how two process design teams were both pursuing the design of a 1 gm microprocessor. One team was based in Oregon and the other in Israel.

The U.S. team went down a path that led to the creation of a very complex processor that wasn't going to work because the unit produced too much heat. In parallel, the Israeli team — composed of male and female leaders from around the world with completely different worldviews — came up with a completely new process that *wasn't* complex. They respected each other for the

---

105 Steve Brown, *The Bald Futurist*. http://www.baldfuturist.com/.

value that each person brought to the table and listened without discounting one another.

As a result, they created a product that ultimately saved the company's future. That's the kind of impact that connecting and collaborating across differences can produce. But, Brown cautions, leaders must master the ability to listen. And valuing others has to become a leadership principle. One way to think about this opportunity, he says, is simply to ask yourself a key question: "Who around you will surprise you with knowledge, insight or experiences that will save you, your team and your company?" If you believe the data I shared in previous chapters about where your growth is going to come from, then every leader should be running to collaborate with women, especially multicultural women.

According to Amy Cuddy's research, people think about competence *after* they have decided if they can trust you. Trust and respect take time to earn and are lost quickly. If we could combine empathy, curiosity, trustworthiness and respect, we might create the kind of leaders who would inherently want to stand up for equality.

Leadership must be centered on serving instead of selfish agendas. No narcissists need apply!

The best starting point is with your own team. I am talking about driving radical inclusion. I am talking about creating a culture where everyone is truly valued and respected, cared for as assets, the status quo can be openly challenged, diversity of thought and style is embraced and accountability thrives.

Mike Solomita, a Vice President at Cisco, refers to the creation of a culture where everyone is all in as *a culture of deep democracy*. I have been blessed to get to know this gentleman and work with him. Solomita shared his story with me:

I have a dear friend and colleague, Molly Tschang. Molly was in my former consulting group — more of a think tank and visionary group. She came and interviewed with me, and I hired her on the spot. It was a match made in heaven.

It was end of the year performance time. I was starting to read the statements my team was writing about how inclusivity was expressed, and I was absolutely embarrassed. So, Molly and I started to explore how we could move the diversity and inclusion needle. I knew from my own life experiences and research that diverse teams perform better. One of the things I did when I was promoted to the VP level was to create "open mic" sessions. I wanted to hear from my team. These sessions were an opportunity for any employee in my scope of responsibility to express their comments or concerns or ask questions. We started to learn that people were willing to use their voice, but we needed to create the environment.

Molly has a long career of leading through change and was certified in the ORSC (Organization and Relationship Systems Coaching) model. She reflected on the type of culture where there was an equal playing field for everyone, and the ORSC "deep democracy" was at the core of what we were trying to achieve, that all voices in the relationship system need to be heard – including the unpopular ones – to accurately represent reality and realize the system's full potential.

Deep democracy is a concept that facilitates all voices being heard — authentically. Remember the framework for America's independence? The second paragraph of the United States' Declaration of Independence starts as follows:

We hold these truths to be self-evident, <u>that all men are created equal</u>, that they are endowed by their Creator with certain unalienable Rights, which among these are Life, Liberty and the Pursuit of Happiness. That to secure these rights, Governments are instituted among Men, deriving their just powers from the consent of the governed.[106]

Despite all our efforts and our authentic commitment, when we first asked to "hear your voice," people were skeptical. Some people were so scarred from previous experiences that they were slow to open up.

I knew that I had to walk the walk, that the senior leader sets the tone for the culture, for how

---

106 The United States Declaration of Independence, 1776.

other leaders lead. I knew that all eyes would be on me. I knew that there were some members of the team who wanted to share, but weren't really sure it was safe. Yet I knew that I had to be vulnerable. I didn't have all the answers about creating a culture of deep democracy, and I said that out loud.

It is important for senior leaders to demonstrate their buy-in so that the energy, sentiment and feeling of equality get passed down to every level. The Cisco organization conducts annual leadership surveys. Instead of picking a few members of my team to be included in the survey, I invited my *entire* team to participate, and I reviewed my results with the entire department. I honestly wanted feedback. I wanted them to see that it was real. I wanted them to see that I was willing to do my own work to show up as a leader who could engage as a person who cared, had high expectations and believed in accountability but who also believed in setting up every member of the team for success.

In addition to the open-mic sessions, we decided to have town hall meetings where the entire team could engage in conversations about their experiences as members of my team. During one of the town hall sessions, a junior-level black male challenged me. He suggested I wasn't demonstrating that I cared under pressure. He shared that from his perspective, I would act like I cared and was open to pushback when things were going well. But in times of stress, I seemed to revert to old behavior patterns. He challenged me to do better.

I really had to use every ounce of my emotional intelligence to hear this feedback and make a commitment to do more. But that's exactly what our people are looking for us to do. They want to know we are building new muscles that will make it easier for them to connect with us.

Over time, people started to believe. Members of the team began to call each other out on behaviors that didn't demonstrate empathy. The team started pointing out bias when it appeared.

It created momentum.

Deep democracy principles connected to the new style of leadership include:

- A willingness to lead with a core belief in *partnership*, not *patriarchy.*
- A willingness to promote and demonstrate total transparency. No hidden agendas.
- A commitment to model inclusive behaviors that send the signal to all employees that they are valued for their differences and that those differences are important and respected.

- Intentionality to create cultures where employees believe they can use their voices to openly call out bias and create "teachable moments" in support of everyone building their cultural competencies.
- A focus on building authentic relationships based upon mutual trust and respect.
- No tolerance for retaliation for members of the team expressing their feelings about their negative experiences as a member of the team.
- A purposeful creation of safe spaces where courageous conversations can occur.
- Create a team agreement that while any problem or concern can be offered, everyone must also offer a possible *solution* to the problem.

In the culture Solomita has created, title doesn't matter. It is a culture where everyone is invited to the table and each voice can be heard because everyone is valued, everyone is respected and everyone is aligned to the experience they want to have with each other. And it is all rooted in the authentic exchange of value.

At the end of the day, to create leaders who are "all in" requires retooling, rethinking and reframing. If you are a leader (male or female) who wants to remain relevant, experience success and expand your impact, you must get all in.

You must stand up for equality. As Hillary Clinton shares, "There cannot be true democracy unless women's voices are heard. There cannot be true democracy unless women are given the opportunity to take responsibility for their own lives. There cannot be true democracy unless all citizens are able to participate fully in the lives of their country."[107]

Getting all in requires each of us to value women and people of color as bright, talented leaders who have something important to bring to the table. Remember, women are directly linked to the future of your business no matter the industry, so the input of female leaders is critical for success.

Are you ready to step up as a leader who believes in equality? Do you really appreciate the impact that making this choice will have on your personal success and your organization's success? If you want to be a part of the future, I need you to stop and reflect on where you stand in regard to moving to a place where you are aligned with the cause from both your head and your heart.

In the words of Ban Ki-moon, the 8th Secretary-General of the United Nations, "Achieving gender equality requires the engagement of women and men, boys and girls. It is everyone's responsibility."[108]

Anyone who works in the business world knows the power of building relationships. The problem is that most women are excluded from developing the kind of

---

107 Hillary Clinton, "Remarks by the First Lady of the United States" (speech, Vital Voices: Woman in Democracy Conference, Austria, Vienna, July 11, 1997).

108 Ban Ki-moon, "International Women's Day 2014: Equality for Women Is Progress for All," (UN General Assembly Event Speech, New York, NY, March 7, 2014).

relationships that will open the door to opportunities. They are not a part of the "club" for all the reasons I have mentioned up to this point in the book. Everything I have written about gives you some sense of what women, particularly women of color, are experiencing in their journey in the business world.

I know you might be thinking, particularly if you are a white male, that women should just step up and form the relationships themselves. If only it were so easy. It takes confidence to attempt to build relationships with members of the dominant group, particularly after trying only to later feel burned and rejected.

I agree that to further their careers all women, particularly women of color, must find the confidence to overcome workplace challenges and build relationships outside their comfort zones.

"Like most [women], multicultural women face challenges personally, interpersonally and organizationally," Audra Bohannon, senior partner at Korn Ferry, told the Network of Executive Women in an interview. "If they are not aware and intentional about how to manage these challenges, they can become less confident in embracing the key requirements of success. They will focus primarily on working hard and will not spend the time required to build strong political, navigational and relationship skills."[109]

---

109 Audra Bohannon, interview by Network of Executive Women Researchers, *Tapestry: Leveraging the Rich Diversity of Women in Retail and Consumer Goods,* 2014.

In many cases, women are helped by managers who offer support in the workplace but who cannot take on the role of a mentor or sponsor — relationships that are absolutely critical to career advancement. To build cross-functional, strategic relationships outside of their managers, women must overcome their reluctance to embrace their vulnerability and reveal who they are as people. They must also closely examine their own unconscious and conscious biases. Were they taught to mistrust members of other groups?

But men must do some things, too. What kind of things, you ask?

To begin, all each of us needs to do is engage in a conversation. Intentionally reach out to a woman, if you are a man; and if you are a woman, reach out to a woman who is not from your culture or your generation and inquire about her career experience.

It's simple. Start with a question: "How has your career experience been different than another woman's or a man's experience from your perspective?" or "What has your experience in the business world been like as a woman?"

Open your mind to learning, to feeling, to understanding what it feels like to not be a member of the dominant group. This style of leadership wants to get out of the office and engage in conversations. This partner leader doesn't shy away from doing what he or she knows should be done. This leader understands that it is not about being clever or even answering the questions. You don't have to make any promises.

All you need to do is create space for a courageous conversation to occur, and then listen.

Now of course you have to enter the conversation with a willingness to listen and understand. It's about a willingness to step into another person's experience. And, for goodness' sake, please don't discount what you hear. You'll damage the relationship from the get-go. Perhaps you are familiar with Theodore Roosevelt's quote, "People don't care how much you know until they know how much you care." That applies perfectly here.

This courageous conversation is all about demonstrating that you care.

Consider the 5 Cs as a framework for your conversations as a partnership leader:

- Courage
- Caring
- Curiosity
- Collaboration
- Conviction

This framework will help you move from a superficial conversation into a meaningful one where you can talk about the other person's experience in terms of race, gender and generation.

I know most people find conversations of this nature to be uncomfortable. It's okay that you are uncomfortable. It's natural. Just lean into it and recognize that if you extend the olive branch, the other party will generally reciprocate.

Stop now and consider. Make the decision to get into the game of driving equality. Next, make a list of five women who you think would be willing to engage in a courageous conversation with you, and speak with at least one of them. Whatever you do or say during the conversation, please don't discount anything she shares. It is her truth. It shouldn't be dismissed or judged. Instead, you must make the commitment to act on the information you receive.

This new style of leader has curiosity at his or her core. They recognize that they are and will be forever learning. Responding to today's new workforce is just another opportunity to learn and remain effective as a leader.

The workplace has changed. The customers have changed. The business landscape has changed. It is now time for the leaders to change.

COURAGEOUS CALL-TO-ACTION REFLECTION QUESTIONS

- Would people describe you as an inclusive leader or an exclusive leader?
- As you look at your team's composition does it suggest you have a bias against a demographic or gender?
- Do you offer assistance to others without regard for how your help for them may benefit you?
- Do you believe that a role of a leader is to partner with his or her employee or to oversee or instruct them?
- Do you value what has been referred to as soft collaboration?
- Do you retain knowledge in an attempt to give yourself more power, or do you freely distribute knowledge?
- Do you believe that all are created equal and should have equal opportunities?

Eight

Courageous Conversations About Reimagining and Creating a New Future

"The future depends on what you
do today."

—GANDHI

ANYTHING IS POSSIBLE

John F. Kennedy addressed the Joint Session of Congress on May 25, 1961, regarding urgent national needs. He asked for an additional $7 billion to $9 billion over the next five years for the space program, stating to Congress:

"This nation should commit itself to achieving the goal, before the decade is out, of landing a man on the moon and returning him safely to the Earth."[110]

---

110 John F. Kennedy, "Special Message to the Congress on Urgent National Needs" (Congressional Address, Washington, D.C., May 25, 1961).

At the time of that statement, skeptics questioned the ability of the National Aeronautics and Space Administration (NASA) to meet Kennedy's schedule. Within a year, however, Alan Shepard and Gus Grissom became the first two Americans to travel into space.[111]

I share this particular story because I want you to understand and believe that it is possible to make major change happen in a short time period if you rally enough people who believe. There is power in numbers. There is power in believers.

I am always inspired when I recall or tell this story. It reminds me that anything is possible if we believe. It also reminds me that when we, as humans, become convicted to make change, things happen.

In the words of Jason Kilar, "There is no adversity capable of stopping you once the choice to persevere is made."[112] It is time for all of us to make that choice and come together to figure out how we partner in advancing the changes that are needed for women and people of color to experience equality in the workplace.

Robin Ely is one of my favorite professors at the Harvard Business School. She has conducted extensive research on gender and leadership. One of the points she repeatedly makes is that to become a leader, you must

111 "Apollo Moon Landing," jfklibrary.org, http://www.jfklibrary.org/JFK/JFK-Legacy/NASA-Moon-Landing.aspx.

112 Jason Kilar, "2015 Spring Commencement Address" (Commencement Address, University of North Carolina at Chapel Hill, NC, May 10, 2015).

internalize a leadership identity. I agree with her assertion that people have to *see* themselves as leaders in order to *become* leaders. I believe the same is true for becoming an agent of change. Women and men need to see themselves as agents of change to drive equality. And hopefully what you have learned is that it requires a deep personal conviction and commitment. Part of seeing yourself as an agent of change requires a commitment to choosing service to others over service to self.

RESPONDING TO CHANGE

In his book *Stewardship: Choosing Service over Self-Interest*, Peter Block suggests that change brings uncertainty and causes people to respond in a variety of ways including the victim, critic, bystander, navigator or charger modes. People who respond in the *victim* mentality resist change and invite drama. They are the quickest to revert to old patterns of doing things. The *critic* looks for reasons as to why the change won't work. The *bystander*, as would be expected, is reluctant to get involved. The *navigator* joins quickly and looks for ways to explain the change and why it is useful. The *charger* often pushes too hard.[113]

Recognizing the various responses to stepping out and offering the bold challenge of gender equality will no doubt stir up several emotions, first felt on a personal

---

113 Peter Block, *Stewardship: Choosing Service over Self-Interest* (California: Berrett-Koehler Publishers, 2013).

level. It is important that you engage in some self-examination to determine if you are truly ready to step out as an agent of change; otherwise you might experience even greater frustration.

Let me explain. There are many scholars who have created change management models. Almost all those models suggest that most people who are charged with leading or managing change start out on an emotional high. As they begin to engage in the process of transforming and changing, their mindset is open. They demonstrate, via their behaviors, that they believe the change can really come to fruition. They are often elated, as John Fisher's model suggests, at the beginning, but as they begin to spread the "good news," they are met with resistance. As a result, they begin to second-guess themselves. Their energy starts to wane. Fear sets in. The "inner chatter" — the itty-bitty pity committee — starts to say things like, "This is harder than I thought." Before they know it, they slip into depression. They no longer have the energy to influence others. The message gets drowned out by doubts and frustration.

Some people are able to successfully work through this state of depression and frustration. As they work through the process, they get reenergized and find determination to revive their commitment to the change management initiative. I believe what enables a person to stick with the desired change is the human spirit and a bias for action. I also believe that each of us must be in the right mindset to forge ahead with a tenacious spirit to achieve the stated goals.

One of the best exercises I can encourage you to do to build self-reliance and self-confidence, and I have mentioned it before, is to spend some time outlining the 10 most defining moments of your life. This is a very powerful exercise and worth the time that you will invest to do it. When we embark upon challenges or we step into a leadership position where we are leading major changes, we can second-guess ourselves. Let me tell you a story communicating what I mean.

My future son-in-law, Ryan, left for Germany on January 2, 2016. He was going there because of his responsibilities as an Army Captain and had decided to leave the military after this tour of duty.

In preparation for making the transition from the military world into the business world, I asked him to do the 10 defining moments exercise. He said he wrote down a couple of things pretty fast, but then he gave himself permission to really think about what he was made of.

I wanted him to see and believe that he has so much to bring to the business world, but I had no idea this exercise would produce such an honest, meaningful and moving recap of his life to date. I have encouraged him to write his own book because he could help so many men who are afraid to speak about insecurities. His defining moments numbers 4 and 5 afford all of us an in-depth understanding of what men go through as they discover their true character.

He starts defining moment number 4 this way:

"And this year's Black Lion Award goes to... Ryan Brence!" At the end of our last practice before the annual Army vs. Navy football game, our head coach, Stan Brock, announced that I was the recipient of that year's Black Lion Award — presented to the Army football player who best exemplified the characteristics of leadership, courage, devotion to duty, self-sacrifice and, above all, an unselfish concern for the team ahead of himself.

While I felt extreme pride and honor in that moment, it almost felt like déjà vu, as it reminded me so much of the time that I had been honored and recognized in front of my peers for the 8th grade American Legion Award. After everyone had congratulated me and expressed their respect, I couldn't help but feel a sense of uneasiness and anxiousness that I was not deserving of the award. I just didn't want to "mess it up." I knew I wasn't perfect, and although I understood that it was okay if I made a mistake in the upcoming huge game, I felt like the stakes were raised much higher because I had attained such a prestigious award as part of something that meant so very much to me.

As I look back, I really do believe I deserved every bit of that award. I ferociously approached every single day of practice and each game with a passion and work ethic that was unmatched. When guys were taking it easy at the end of practice, when things were more relaxed, there I was, with my motor still running 100 miles per hour looking to do anything in my power to help the team and myself become better. I would stay after practice and work on my technique, condition myself to be in the best shape possible and help whichever teammate needed assistance with the playbook to ensure they felt confident going onto the field. I loved the game, and it gave me an identity while at West Point. I was by no means the star player, but I prided myself on being the hardest worker on the field and in the film room while also being a teammate everyone could count on. With all those awesome qualities, you'd think it would just make me more confident in my overall presence and personal perception.

However, I was still insecure and maintained a nagging fear of "being found out" that I wasn't really that great of a leader… or really that great of a teammate in general. I just couldn't accept the award deep down, and I remember that really bothering me. Yet, to this day, I will always count the Black Lion Award as the biggest honor in my life because it represented four years of extreme hard work, dedication and passion towards the sport I grew up playing and absolutely loved.

I was being recognized for the person football had helped me become, but I couldn't accept myself if it was all stripped away. What was I really looking for to attain peace and joy in who I was, *aside from the awards or recognition? Well, I was about to find out in one of the hardest ways possible that would leave me with no other choice but to accept myself for who I was — not based on merit or through the viewpoint of others, but rather based on my true identity given to me through the Creator of this world.*

If you are a believer, you know you and I were created by the Creator of the universe. You also believe that you are here for a purpose. You and I have work to do while we are on this earth. And doing this work requires us to make a choice. Ryan's fifth defining moment demonstrates the power of choice:

Ranger School was, and most likely always will be, the most excruciating physical, mental, emotional and spiritual experience I have ever undergone in my life. Being an athlete, I had endured many agonizing days of training and competition, but attending Ranger School during the heat of summer in Georgia and in the swamps of Florida proved to be a true test of my strength, endurance, psyche and faith.

After the first phase of Ranger School at Fort Benning, Georgia, I set out to the mountains of Northern Georgia with my platoon of Rangers to endure arguably the toughest of the three phases of Ranger School. At the beginning of this phase, since we would be traversing many mountains, we were required to learn basic rappelling skills. Just like everything else in Ranger School, pressure was associated with learning the required tasks given to each student. Out of all the things I could have failed in Ranger School, it was rappel rope-knot tying that I missed the mark on. Knot-tying, for God's sake! Due to the annual Best Ranger Competition being held at that time, the school was put on hold for a month and a half while I was recycled, which meant I had to wait until the next class started up again to resume my participation in the course.

I was so discouraged during this time and lacked all confidence, stemming from my experience and self-perceived poor performance in the school up to that point, that I made up my mind I was going to quit and sign the necessary Lack of Motivation (LOM) Memorandum needed to leave Ranger School (yes, they actually give the paperwork an official demoralizing title).

The night before I was to sign my paperwork, I was lying down in my bunk in the corner of the barracks having a pity party when I kept hearing someone talk about God from across the room. I don't know exactly what he was discussing, but all I know is that I kept hearing the all-powerful word and was somehow drawn to it.

As I made my way over to the sound of the voice, I witnessed a passionate yet self-controlled man talking about his relationship with God. He was speaking to a bitter, brutal man who was claiming to be an atheist. Picking up a book to make it seem like I was simply reading within the vicinity of their conversation, I listened to Chris (as I later found out his name to be) speak to the other agitated, impatient man. He spoke with love and patience as the atheist belittled each and every one of his claims.

Finally, the atheist stormed out of the conversation after calling Chris ridiculous for believing in such a ridiculous set of ideas. At this point, Chris's attention quickly shifted over to me as I was sitting nearby him. I was "reading" a book that was upside down, unbeknownst to me at the time. Chuckling, Chris sarcastically asked me what it was that I was reading, and after an awkward exchange of glances, he introduced himself to me.

After a couple of minutes of small talk, Chris got right down to the heart of the matter and asked me what was going on. For whatever reason, I felt compelled and completely comfortable in telling Chris exactly how I was feeling in the moment and my plans to leave Ranger School the following day. Chris asked me about my relationship with God, and I told him about my belief in Him but also about the unrelenting void in my heart that I was searching to fill through validation and security from all the wrong sources.

Chris took me outside of the barracks. As soon as we left the building, a Ranger School instructor rushed up to us and fiercely asked what we were doing, and Chris quickly replied to him that we were heading to get our laundry from the facility just across the street.

After the encounter, Chris looked at me and told me that he honestly believed what had just transpired could have easily been a potential assault on what was about to occur.

What was about to occur ended up being Chris taking me into the laundry room, not to wash clothes but rather to talk to me about God and a relationship with Him. I ultimately had to make the decision to either stay at Ranger School and pursue a relationship with Him while being mentored by Chris or go back to Fort Hood and begin my Army career after a short-lived, disappointing Ranger School experience.

I ended up deciding to stick it out. For the next month, Chris and I met every single day in the same laundry room to read the Bible, talk about God and pray. Naturally, every day while we were having our Bible study, other Ranger students would come into the laundry room to wash and dry their clothes. They would notice us with our Bibles open, talking about God. It would always make me a little bit uncomfortable, but Chris welcomed the interest and intrigue of each soldier who was curious as to what we were up to, in the laundry room of all places.

After a couple of weeks, our two-man Bible study grew to five Rangers to 10 Rangers and then even more. It was a chain-reaction domino effect, and what a blessing it was for all of us — including Chris — as he would constantly give glory to God for His incredible work in the hearts of many of whom we would consider to be tough, independent guys.

When the time came to start up Ranger School again, I was nervous about going back into "the suck" (as we all called it), but I had a new relationship and faith in the Lord to see me through it all no matter what the outcome would be. The school did not get any easier with my new faith, but there was a peace that came along with the stress and physical pain that I hadn't experienced beforehand. Even in the most critical times when I knew I was being heavily evaluated and scrutinized for my every move and command, I was able to be in the moment, think clearly, and execute to the best of my abilities with God at my side. Even with some slip-ups, I was able to eventually pass my missions (and tie my knots!) and graduate from arguably the hardest school in the military.

A couple of days before graduation, I went to a chapel service led by a Ranger chaplain. In that service, he gave us the opportunity to be baptized on graduation day if any of us felt led to do so. I remember there being many hands raised to commit to this idea. On graduation day, however, there were only three at the site. I was one of those three. Immediately following the Ranger School graduation, with my family there to witness my baptism, I told the crowd of people what an impact the school had made on me in more ways than one. Ultimately, I knew God had me right where He wanted me the whole time, and I couldn't imagine a better way to end my journey than giving all the glory to Him and being baptized by being immersed in water in the name of Jesus Christ.

That day symbolized a huge turning point in my life as I freely made the decision to follow Christ knowing that I had given my life to Him. While the road ahead would still remain arduous, and even tougher at times than before, I knew that I was a child of God destined to become more like Christ with each and every challenge that would arise.[114]

I am so proud of Ryan. He is such a great man. Mike and I both feel so blessed to know that our daughter is marrying a man of such strength, depth and, yes, power.

Wouldn't it be great if we operated in cultures where we could be this vulnerable and transparent about our

---

114 Ryan Brence in a discussion with the author, May 2016.

feelings without fear of it being used against us? Wouldn't it be great if, when we were waning in our beliefs about ourselves, that someone like Chris would come by our side?

We all need a Chris so that we stay with the challenge that is before us.

We need to find a way — as Ryan did — to pull ourselves out of the emotional hole of "I can't do this," as we encounter barriers to our success. And we must move from the dreaded drama triangle into the winner's triangle.

If we can stand firm in the face of change and uncertainty, momentum will pick back up and we will become stronger and more convicted. Instead of retreating into old behavior patterns, we become convinced that we can transform and achieve our stated goals.

All of us know what it is like to set a goal for personal change. And all of us know how easy it is to backtrack and slip back into old habits.

So, what am I saying? It is not enough to start the change. Change agents have to be tenacious and resilient to accomplish the goal. You must know *what* you stand for and *why* you stand for it. It has to burn in your belly. You have to want it so much that you dream about it. You wake up thinking about ways you can advance the cause.

While this change process may begin at the *mind* level, it is fulfilled in the *spirit* level. I have heard it said, "The human brain is limited, but the human spirit is limitless."

I believe this is very true. My life experiences growing up in the deep South during times of segregation certainly didn't lend well to me believing I could do anything more than go to a trade school. At least that's what the people around me developed as a narrative given I was a black girl. But my spirit knew differently. My spirit would convince me that anything was possible.

My mother, God rest her soul, used to tell me that there was no such word as "can't." "Take it out of your vocabulary" was what I heard every time I used it, and, over time, I started to catch myself as I would begin to use the word. I replaced the word "can't" with something like, "It may be a challenge, but I am up for the challenge."

So many times in my life I have spoken those words to myself!

Are you up for the challenge of leading the change for gender equality? Believe in yourself.

THE POWER OF THE HUMAN SPIRIT

When in corporate, I was a member of a senior leadership team. There were roughly 20 of us. I was the only woman and, of course, the only woman of color. We earned a reputation for being a group with high standards. We also earned a reputation for being a tough group to convince to change or support new initiatives.

Truth be told, we loved new initiatives, but we wanted to make sure that the person leading the change was convicted. We knew how easy it was to create a great idea and how challenging it could be to execute that great idea.

Once a month we would have members of the various departments present new ideas to us. We, like all executives, were all about growing the business, driving efficiency and increasing productivity. So, if someone had a good idea, there was a process to help advance it.

They would have to present it to us in an effort to obtain our endorsement before budget dollars would be allocated to the cause, and we would intentionally challenge anyone who came into the boardroom to present ideas, findings, initiatives, etc. No matter how positive we felt about what was being presented, we would drill the person and challenge the data. We would poke holes in the ideas. We would throw up barriers to explain why the idea wouldn't work.

We created tension to test the individual. Those who were convicted leaned into the tension. They recognized that creating something new, advancing change or challenging conventional thinking required a willingness to stand alone momentarily. These leaders understood that part of getting others to buy in to a new idea requires them to stand firm, without apology, and demonstrate a belief that was so solid, nothing we said could tear down their convictions.

Only those leaders who stood strong would make it to our last question: "Are you willing to die on the sword for what you say you believe?"

It's that kind of human spirit that makes things happen. The power of the human spirit manifests itself any time a human being encounters a challenge beyond what is ordinarily experienced, accomplishes something that has never been done before or perseveres against insurmountable odds. We all have been in a place where we are the first to have done something.

Derek Sivers in his 2010 TED Talk, "How to Start a Movement," says it always takes a person, a leader, to step out and take that first step.[115] Sometimes in taking that first step, a leader has to stand alone for a while as an innovator until he or she can convince the first follower to come. The first follower then creates other followers and so on. These followers become role models. As others watch these role models, they join as followers that are totally bought in. They come with excitement, energy and passion to the same degree of the first follower. A movement begins with a courageous leader challenging the status quo.

While Sivers suggests that the bold leaders who step out show others how to follow, *how* we show up in the corporate world can be the model for others. We don't have to buy in to becoming an ego-driven leader. We can instead be a serving leader. We don't have to use stereotypes that hurt others. We can be leaders who are known for developing other leaders because we believe that *every* person has value.

Stepping out to create business worlds where every employee can thrive requires us to be willing to go first.

Bill Gates models what it means to stand alone in conviction.

---

115 Derek Sivers, "How to Start a Movement," (TED Talk, 2010).

He could have picked any problem or change in the world to take on, but what did he choose? Malaria — a mosquito-borne infectious disease of humans and other animals caused by parasitic protozoans. It appears mainly in Saharan Africa. Even though malaria is preventable and treatable, the mosquito-borne disease killed 584,000 people in 2013, with 90% of the deaths occurring in sub-Saharan Africa. Of the victims, 83% were children under the age of five. The World Health Organization lists malaria as the fifth biggest killer in sub-Saharan Africa.[116]

The Gates foundation invested $200 million to produce the world's first malaria vaccine. And I can boil it down to one explanation as to why — moral emotions. His spirit was stirred to make a difference in the lives of others.

"Innovation is a good thing. The human condition — put aside bioterrorism and a few footnotes — is improving because of innovation," he said. "But while technology's amazing, it doesn't get down to the people most in need in anything near the timeframe we should want it to."[117]

It is perceptions such as this that have led Gates to spend not just his fortune but most of his time on good works. Other billionaires may take to philanthropy almost as a mark of their social status, but for Gates, it has the force of a moral imperative.

---

116 World Health Organization, *World Malaria Report 2014*, 2014.
117 Bill Gates, interview by Richard Waters, *Financial Times*, November 1, 2013.

The decision to throw himself into causes like trying to prevent childhood deaths in the developing world or improving education in the U.S. was the result of careful ethical calculations. Moral emotions, sometimes referred to as "self-conscious emotions" or "positive moral emotions," are the emotions that conjure up sympathy for others or for what we see happening to others.

Mark Leary, Jeffrey Stuewig and Debra Mashek cite two requirements for feeling a "self-conscious" emotion:

One, the person needs to be capable of "position taking," of knowing how his/her behaviors would affect or be perceived by others. Two, he/she needs the ability to imagine how the reception of his/her behavior would reflect back on her character.[118]

Their research further suggests that these emotions work together like a symphony. Said differently, people will know if you are real. People will be able to tell if you have authentic passion for the work. And they will react accordingly.

Everyone knows the feeling of being in a meeting where a contentious topic is being discussed. There is

---

118 Illana Simons, "The Four Moral Emotions: Guilt, Shame, Embarrassment, and Pride Make Societies Work," *Psychology Today* (blog), November 15, 2009.
https://www.psychologytoday.com/blog/the-literary-mind/200911/the-four-moral-emotions.

pithy debate after which everyone agrees to the final decision. Shortly after the meeting ends, one manager is approached by a member of his team about the outcome. When asked about the final decision, the manager says, "Well, they decided we would..."

As soon as he says, "they," it's over. Employees know when their managers have not bought in to an idea, and they know it is based upon the emotions that manager displays about what he or she believes.

Here's the good news: "Our brains are wired to be kind,"[119] according to Dacher Keltner.

I have always believed, generally speaking, that people *want* to do the right thing. We just have to show them *how*.

STANDING TALL

I don't want any of you to think I believe what I'm asking you to do is easy. Nor will it happen quickly. If it were easy, then the numbers would be dramatically different in favor of women and people of color.

It takes a conscious effort to become an agent of change.

Part of that effort includes recognizing that the choices and decisions you make will not only impact you but also others. In fact, the decisions we make today about gender equality will impact generations who will come behind us.

---

119 Dacher Keltner, "The Compassionate Instinct," *The Greater Good* (2004). http://greatergood.berkeley.edu/article/item/the_compas sionate_instinct/.

Think about advancing this change as a part of your life's work. It's the work that speaks beyond passion into your soul. It allows you, if you accept the invitation, to serve as a role model worth following.

People use the words "role model" loosely. I think they are powerful words with intent and impact. Your life's work is about changing lives. It is not about creating products or innovating products. It is not about your name appearing on a building.

Trust me, people see the names on buildings, and it is a fleeting thought. It's not the building, it's what happens because the building stands and because of the people in that building who are served.

Will you accept the invitation to serve as a true role model?

Will you become an early adopter of a new style of leadership that is committed to equality and willing to put everything on the line to make it become a reality?

Each and every one of us has the power to move the needle on equality. Each of us has an inner creator that, when unleashed, knows we were put on this earth to make an impact upon the lives of others.

At the end of the day, the inner creator is connected to one's life experiences. I am talking about resilience, tenacity, toughness, risk-taking, courage and the experiences that make you who you are.

It's the stuff that makes you stick with a situation even when it is tough.

It's what comforts you at night when you think you can't do any more or take any more.

It's the antidote to self-doubt.

It's self-reliance, self-confidence and faith that convince us we can do things we never imagined.

Our challenge as we make a commitment to do this important work is to dig deep and show the world what we are made of. As long as we hold back, as long as we go along to get along, as long as we turn our heads, things will remain the same.

We must understand that what we do with our gifts and talents requires us to make a choice, an intentional choice. I am asking every person who dares to read this book to recognize that our choices empower us to be game changers.

We must choose to use our voice to say that equality should be a reality. For ALL people. We may not all be destined to achieve greatness as the world defines it — money, wealth, material goods — but we are great and can have great impact even if it is changing only one person's life.

BABY STEPS THAT LEAD TO A MOVEMENT

It's time for you to make a decision about your role in advancing gender equality.

It's time to put up or shut up.

If you have never read the book *The Art of Possibility* by Rosamund Stone Zander and Benjamin Zander, you should put it on your short list of books to read. The key message in this book is straightforward. The authors suggest that possibility thinking is the management of ideas. This book has been used by many leaders to move themselves and their people into a space of innovation and creativity. The authors suggest that we have to speak possibility. It has to become a way of engaging.

In Zander's words, "To speak possibility you do not need to be the top guy in the elegant suit. You can speak possibility from any position, in any group of people, anywhere in the world. This leader keeps a possibility alive until every person involved in the project is enrolled in it."[120]

I also believe that it is critical for us to imagine a world where equality exists. Imagination is critical to possibility thinking. We have to see it in our head and feel it in our hearts so it will manifest itself. We have to speak it out to others. Every one of us needs to start seeing and speaking gender equality. It needs to be at the top of the list for your business discussions, talent discussions and sustainability discussions.

Impossibility thinkers (naysayers) are the folks who, at the first suggestion of a new idea, cut it down. They are negative. They drain the energy from those around them.

One of my favorite thought leaders is John Kotter. He has written several books on change, one titled *Buy In*, about how to save a good idea from getting shut down.

---

120 Rosamund Stone Zander, Benjamin Zander, *The Art of Possibility* (New York: Penguin Books, 2000).

Kotter argues that the thing a leader must do to protect his or her idea is to understand the unfair attack strategies that naysayers, nitpickers and handwringers deploy with great success time and time again.

Said differently, we must anticipate that driving equality is not going to be the number-one priority for everyone. And, honestly, there is going to be a group of people who don't want it to happen, period. We know they are coming, so we must do what Kotter is suggesting. We must study their patterns and figure out how to overcome their reactions as barriers. At the end of the day, if we don't truly believe it, it will be so easy for anyone to tear down the idea of equality.

The term "possibility thinking" (PT), was originally coined by Craft (1999) to represent a process which may be common across life, as well as across differing levels of generative activity, from "little c" to "big c" creativity.[121]

Developed initially in conceptual work, it was encapsulated as the posing of the question "What if?" in different ways and contexts, together with perspective taking, or "As if" thinking. To this degree, it was argued that PT could be seen as involving the shift from "What is this and what does it do?" to "What can I or we do with this?" [122]

---

121 Anna Craft, "Creativity and Possibility in the Early Years," *Research Paper.* http://www.tactyc.org.uk/pdfs/Reflection-craft.pdf.
122 Centre for Research in Education and Educational Technology, The Open University, *Possibility Thinking*, 2012. https://www.open.ac.uk/creet/main/sites/www.open.ac.uk.creet.main/files/06%20Possibility%20Thinking.pdf.

Let me share some examples of possibility thinkers.

Everyone knows of Martin Luther King, Jr., but few people know of Benjamin Mays. Mays was a possibility thinker. He was a mentor to a number of people, including Dr. King. Benjamin Elijah Mays was an American Baptist minister, activist, humanitarian and leader in the African-American Civil Rights Movement. He was born in the 1890s — the youngest of eight children born to Louvenia Carter and Hezekiah Mays, tenant farmers and former slaves — in a rural area outside Ninety-Six, South Carolina.

A consistent theme in Mays' boyhood and early adulthood was his quest for education against overwhelming odds. He refused to be limited by the widespread poverty and racism of his place of birth. After some struggle, he gained acceptance to Bates College in Maine. After completing his B.A. there in 1920, Mays entered the University of Chicago as a graduate student, earning an M.A. in 1925 and a Ph.D. in the School of Religion in 1935.

Mays is best known for his role in the advancement of civil rights and the progression of political rights of African Americans. He was active working with world leaders such as John F. Kennedy, Martin Luther King, Jr. and John D. Rockefeller in improving the social standing of minorities in politics, education and business.

Mays was the President of Morehouse College where King was a student in seminary school. It was Mays who influenced King to think about Christianity as a way to advance social change for equality. He sowed a seed of possibility for achievements that would fundamentally change American history.

You and I can be a modern-day Benjamin Mays.

A lot of people know of Rosa Parks, but few people know about the seed sower who came *before* Rosa Parks. Her name was Claudette Colvin.

Colvin was a pioneer of the African-American Civil Rights Movement. She was a 15-year-old girl who refused to give up her seat to a white man on a Montgomery city bus in violation of local law. Claudette Colvin was arrested and taken to jail.

She shared, "As a teenager, I kept thinking, 'Why don't the adults around here just say something? Say it so that they know we don't accept segregation!' I knew then and I know now that, when it comes to justice, there is no easy way to get it. You can't sugarcoat it. You have to take a stand and say, 'This is not right.' And I did."[123]

Nine months later, Rosa Parks made history when she refused to sit at the back of the bus. Colvin was the one who served as the example for Rosa Parks. She made it less risky to stand up for justice. And if we slow down enough to reflect on history, we will find countless other examples of leaders who were seed sowers. They were the first, or the first follower. They made the risk easier for those who came behind them.

And then there's Susan B. Anthony.

---

123 Phillip Hoose, *Claudette Colvin: Twice Toward Justice* (New York: Square Fish, 2009).

In February 1906, Susan B. Anthony made her last speech at a convention in Baltimore. She told the women, "I am here for a little time only, and then my place will be filled...the fight must not cease. You must see that it does not stop. Failure is impossible."[124]

She was given a 10-minute ovation.

You or I may not be a Susan B. Anthony, a Martin Luther King, Jr., a Rosa Parks or a Mother Teresa, but we *all* can be an inspiration and can contribute to moving the needle.

You may move the needle in your world by intentionally creating mentoring circles for women who are not as advanced in their careers. Someone else may move it by sponsoring a woman of color into the boardroom. Or another might move the needle by fighting for work-life balance policies.

Everybody just has to do their fair share.

I am asking you to commit to doing more for others than you are now. I know you might be saying or thinking, "Sure, I mentor others." Okay, so make sure you mentor across differences and ethnicities.

We need to start taking baby steps to become more competent and confident. Baby steps can lead to a movement. Will Smith — yes, the former "Fresh Prince of Bel Air" — gave the world some great advice about facing

---

124 Susan B. Anthony, "Failure Is Impossible," (speech, Suffrage Hearings, Washington, D.C., February 15, 1906).

the future during his interview with Charlie Rose about his accomplishments and success.

When asked about his outlook, he simply said, "You don't try to build a wall, you don't set out to build a wall. You don't say, 'I'm gonna build the biggest, baddest wall that's ever been built.' You say, 'I'm gonna lay this brick, as perfectly as a brick can be laid,' and you do that every single day, and soon you have a wall. It's difficult to take the first step when you look how big the task is. The task is never huge to me, it's always one brick." [125]

Building on his sentiments, I think each of us has to be convinced that if we do our part day in and day out, then we can build something big *together*. I was personally inspired by this interview. What resonated with me in the most powerful way was his desire to represent possibilities. I love that. I want to represent possibilities. I want my life to mean something to others. I think we all do. But to do so, we must live to serve.

There is value to having women and people of color at all levels in any organization. In 2013, Warren Buffett made a bold statement during his interview at CNN. "Fellow males, get on board."[126]

125 Will Smith, interview by Charlie Rose, *Charlie Rose,* PBS, March 13, 2002. https://www.youtube.com/watch?v=jwxlYMmQu9Q.

126 Warren Buffett, interview by Poppy Harlow, *CNN Money,* CNN, June 17, 2013. http://money.cnn.com/video/news/2013/06/17/n-warren-buffett-women-in-business-full.cnnmoney/.

The closer America comes to fully employing the talents of *all* its citizens, the greater its output of goods and services will be. We've seen what can be accomplished when we use 50% of our human capacity. If you visualize what 100% can do, then you'll join me in unbridled optimism about America's future.

More leaders need to stand up and step out as agents of change in full support and advocacy. Moving the needle to advance representation, fair pay and equal opportunities for women and all people of color comes down to one word: LEADERSHIP.

Our choices empower us to be game changers.

Are you ready to stand up and take the pledge to be a leader who believes in EQUALITY?

Only you can make the choice to be part of a movement that ensures that your children will be able to work in organizations where everyone is valued no matter their gender or ethnicity.

May your page in history say that you were a courageous leader who was willing to take on the big issues not because it was popular, but because your conscience knew the difference between right and wrong.

COURAGEOUS CALL-TO-ACTION REFLECTION QUESTIONS

- Will you remain a part of the silent majority or will you find the courage to act?
- Have you thought about your legacy?
- Are you open to being enriched?
- Do you know what it feels like to be an outsider and long for someone to open the door?
- When your career is over will you have been a champion for equality or will others say you didn't care?
- When you breathe your last breath, will you know that you did everything in your power to leave it better than you found it?

Selected Bibliography

Alliance for Board Diversity. *Missing Pieces: Women and Minorities on Fortune 500 Boards—2010 Alliance for Board Diversity Census*. Revised July 21, 2011. http://theabd.org/abd_report.pdf.

Angyal, Chloe. "Affirmative Action Is Great for White Women. So Why Do They Hate It?" *Huffington Post*, January 21, 2016, updated June 23, 2016. http://www.huffingtonpost.com/entry/affirmative-action-white-women_us_56a0ef6ae4b0d8cc1098d3a5).

Anthony, Susan B. "Failure Is Impossible." Speech at the Suffrage Hearings, Washington, D.C., February 15, 1906.

"Apollo Moon Landing." Jfklibrary.org. http://www.jfklibrary.org/JFK/JFK-Legacy/NASA-Moon-Landing.aspx.

Berdahl, Jennifer, and Cameron Anderson. "Women More Collaborative in Work Teams." *Group Dynamics: Theory, Research and Practice*. March 2005.

Block, Peter. *Stewardship: Choosing Service over Self-Interest*. California: Berrett-Koehler Publishers, 2013.

Bohannon, Audra. *Tapestry: Leveraging the Rich Diversity of Women in Retail and Consumer Goods.* Interview by Network of Executive Women Researchers, 2014.

Buffett, Warren. *CNN Money.* By Poppy Harlow. CNN, June 17, 2013. http://money.cnn.com/video/news/2013/06/17/n-warren-buffett-women-in-business-full.cnnmoney/.

Burns, Crosby, K. Barton and S. Kerby. "The State of Diversity in Today's Workforce Report." *The Center for American Progress.* July 12, 2012. https://www.americanprogress.org/issues/economy/reports/2012/07/12/11938/the-state-of-diversity-in-todays-workforce/.

Catalyst. *2005 Catalyst Member Benchmarking Report.* 2005. http://www.catalyst.org/system/files/2005MemberBenchmarkingReport.pdf.

Centre for Research in Education and Educational Technology. The Open University. *Possibility Thinking.* 2012. https://www.open.ac.uk/creet/main/sites/www.open.ac.uk.creet.main/files/06%20Possibility%20Thinking.pdf.

Chen, Joy. *Tapestry: Leveraging the Rich Diversity of Women in Retail and Consumer Goods.* Interview by Network of Executive Women Researchers, 2014.

Clance, Pauline, and Suzanne Imes. "The Imposter Phenomenon in High Achieving Women: Dynamics and Therapeutic Intervention." *Psychotherapy: Theory, Research and Practice* 15, no. 3 (1978).

Craft, Anna. "Creativity and Possibility in the Early Years." Research Paper. http://www.tactyc.org.uk/pdfs/Reflection-craft.pdf.

Cunningham, Lillian. "Cathy Engelbert on Becoming Deloitte's First Female CEO." *Washington Post*, March 20, 2015.

Deggans, Eric. "It's Called 'Africa.' Of Course It's About Race, Right?" *National Public Radio*, December 16, 2013. http://www.npr.org/sections/codeswitch/2013/12/16/251622850/it-s-called-africa-of-course-it-s-about-race-right. Accessed May 2, 2017.

Deloitte. *Global Human Capital Trends 2014.* https://dupress.deloitte.com/dup-us-en/focus/human-capital-trends/2014.html?icid=hp:ft:01.

Dover, Tessa L., Brenda Major, and Cheryl R. Kaiser. "Diversity Policies Rarely Make Companies Fairer, and They Feel Threatening to White Men." *Harvard Business Review*. January 4, 2016.

Duan, Changming Duan. "Being empathic: The role of motivation to empathize and the nature of target emotions." *Motivation and Emotion* 24, no. 1, 2000.

Duan, Changming, and Clara E. Hill. "The Current State of Empathy Research." *Journal of Counseling Psychology* 43, no. 3 (1996).

Dweck, Carol. *Mindset: The New Psychology of Success.* New York: Ballentine Books, 2006.

Einstein, Albert. *Only Then Shall We Find Courage.* Emergency Committee of Atomic Scientists, 1946.

Fukunaga, Cary Joji. *Beasts of No Nation*. Film. Directed by Cary Joji Fukunaga. 2015. Venice: Red Crown Productions, Primary Productions, Parliament of Owls, Bleeker Street, Netflix, 2015. Film and streaming.

Gates, Bill. *Financial Times.* By Richard Waters. November 1, 2013.

Goleman, Daniel. *Working with Emotional Intelligence.* New York: Bantam Dell, 2000.

Goudreau, Jenna. "A Harvard Psychologist Says People Judge You Based on Two Criteria When They First Meet You." *Business Insider Australia*, 2016. http://www.businessinsider.com.au/harvard-psychologist-amy-cuddy-how-people-judge-you-2016-1?r=US&IR=T.

Greenwald, Tony, Mahzarin Banaji, Brian Nosek, Bethany Teachman and Matt Nock. "Project Implicit." *Harvard University*, 2011. https://implicit.harvard.edu/implicit/.

Hammer, Mitchell R., in conjunction with Intercultural Development Inventory, LLC. "Organization – Sample Individual Profile Report." *Intercultural Development v. 3(IDI)*. 2012. https://idiinventory.com/wp-content/themes/evolution/pdfs/Jose_-_Exemplar_-_Profile_-_August_2012.pdf.

Hammer, Mitchell R., Milton J. Bennett and Richard Wiseman. "Measuring Intercultural Sensitivity: The Intercultural Development Inventory." *International Journal of Intercultural Relations* 27, no. 4 (2003).

Hewlett, Sylvia Ann, Kerrie Peraino, Laura Sherbin and Karen Sumburg. "The Sponsor Effect: Breaking Through the Last Glass Ceiling." *The Harvard Business Review Research Report*, December 2010.

Hillary Clinton. "Remarks by the First Lady of the United States." Speech at the Vital Voices: Woman in Democracy Conference, Austria, Vienna, July 11, 1997.

Hoose, Phillip. *Claudette Colvin: Twice Toward Justice.* New York: Square Fish, 2009.

Humphreys, Jeffrey Matthew. *The Multicultural Economy 2008.* Athens, GA: Selig Center for Economic Growth, Terry College of Business, University of Georgia, 2008.

Huppke, Rex. "The Harm of Mansplaining at Work." *Chicago Tribune*, May 13, 2016. http://www.chicagotribune. com/business/careers/ijustworkhere/ct-huppke-work-advice-mansplaining-0515-biz-20160512-column.html.

Halter, Jeffery Tobias. "The 4 Core Values of Millennial Women." *Newonline.org.* http://www.newonline.org/ news/259642/The-4-core-values-of-Millennial-women.htm.

Kang, Jerry. "Implicit Bias: A Primer for Courts," August 2009. http://jerrykang.net/research/2009-implicit-bias-primer-for-courts/.

Kellett, Janet B., Ronald H. Humphrey, Randall G. Sleeth. "Empathy and the Emergence of Task and Relations Leaders." *Leadership Quarterly* 17, 2006.

Keltner, Dacher. "The Compassionate Instinct." *The Greater Good* (2004). http://greatergood.berkeley.edu/article/item/the_compassionate_instinct/.

Kennedy, John F. "Special Message to the Congress on Urgent National Needs." Congressional Address, Washington, D.C., May 25, 1961.

Kent, Muhtar. "This Century Goes to the Women. *Huffington Post*. http://www.huffingtonpost.com/muhtar-kent/post_1057_b_762044.html.

Kilar, Jason. "2015 Spring Commencement Address." Commencement Address, University of North Carolina at Chapel Hill, NC, May 10, 2015.

Ki-moon, Ban. "International Women's Day 2014: Equality for Women Is Progress for All." UN General Assembly Event Speech, New York, NY, March 7, 2014.

LeanIn.org and McKinsey & Co. *Women in the Workplace Report 2016*, 2016. https://womenintheworkplace.com/.

Martin, Andre. "The Changing Nature of Leadership." *A CCL Research White Paper*, 2007. http://www.ccl.org/wp-content/uploads/2015/04/NatureLeadership.pdf.

McGregor, Jena. "This Staggering Chart Shows How Few Minority Women Hold Executive Positions." *Washington Post*, March 30, 2016. https://www.washingtonpost.com/news/on-leadership/wp/2016/03/30/this-staggering-chart-shows-how-few-minority-women-hold-executive-positions/?utm_term=.51fca2483cbc.

McIntosh, Peggy. "White Privilege: Unpacking the Invisible Knapsack." *Peace and Freedom Magazine.* July/August 1989.

"The Men, the Myths, the Legends: Why Millennial 'Dudes' Might Be More Receptive to Marketing than We Thought." *Nielsen.com.* December 10, 2014. http://www.nielsen.com/us/en/insights/news/2014/the-men-the-myths-the-legends-why-millennial-dudes-might-be-more-receptive-to-marketing.html.

Mulhere, Kaitlin. "How Wednesday's Supreme Court Case Could Change College Affirmative Action." *Time*, December 8, 2015. http://time.com/money/4140410/preview-fisher-texas-supreme-court-affirmative-action/.

Network of Executive Women Consumer Products/Retail. *Tapestry: Leveraging the Rich Diversity of Women in Retail and Consumer Goods.* 2014. http://workforceexcellence.com/wp-content/uploads/2015/06/Tapestry_Leveraging_Women.pdf.

Nooyi, Indra. *Performance with Purpose*. By Judith McKenna. Walmart Women's Forum 2015. http://corporate.walmart.com/global-womens-forum#.

Padir, Karen Tegan. "Software — and a Woman — at the Heart of Lunar Triumph." *Wired*. https://www.wired.com/insights/2014/08/software-woman-heart-lunar-triumph/.

Pew Research Center. *Women and Leadership: What Makes a Good Leader, and Does Gender Matter?* 2015. http://www.pewsocialtrends.org/2015/01/14/chapter-2-what-makes-a-good-leader-and-does-gender-matter/.

Piazza, Jo. "Women of Color Hit a 'Concrete Ceiling' in Business." *Wall Street Journal*, September 27, 2016. (https://www.wsj.com/articles/women-of-color-hit-a-concrete-ceiling-in-business-1474963440).

Portalatin, Julio A. "The Role of Men: Leading the Charge Together." Presentation at the World Economic Forum Annual Meeting, Davos, Switzerland, January 20, 2016.

Powell, John A. "Reading Between the Lines: Uncovering Unconscious Bias." Presentation at the Unconscious Bias Panel sponsored by the Writers Guild of America West, Screen Actors Guild, Americans for American Values and the Kirwan Institute, Los Angeles, CA, September 30, 2009.

Reardon, Kathleen Kelley. "7 Things to Say When a Conversation Turns Negative." *Harvard Business Review,* May 11, 2016.

Sanchez, Ray, and Laura Smith-Spark. "Two Women Make Army Ranger History." *CNN,* updated August 21, 2015. http://www.cnn.com/2015/08/21/us/women-army-ranger-graduation/index.html.

Sandberg, Sheryl, and Adam Grant. "Speaking While Female." *New York Times,* January 12, 2015. https://www.nytimes.com/2015/01/11/opinion/sunday/speaking-while-female.html?_r=0.

Shapiro, Johanna. "How do physicians teach empathy in the primary care setting?" *Academic Medicine* 77, 4, 2002.

Sivers, Derek. "How to Start a Movement" TED Talk, 2010. https://www.ted.com/talks/derek_sivers_how_to_start_a_movement.

Smith, Will. *Charlie Rose.* By Charlie Rose. PBS, March 13, 2002. https://www.youtube.com/watch?v=jwxlYMmQu9Q.

Society of Human Resource Managers (SHRM). *SHRM Survey Findings: Diversity and Inclusion.* April 8, 2014. https://www.shrm.org/hr-today/trends-and-forecasting/research-and-surveys/pages/diversity-inclusion.aspx.

Staines, G.L., T.E. Jayaratn, and C. Tavris, "The Queen Bee Syndrome." In *The Female Experience,* ed. C. Tavris. Del Mar, CA: CRM Books, 1973.

Stier, Haya, and Meir Yaish. "Occupational Segregation and Gender Inequality and Job Quality: A Multi-Level Approach." *Work, Employment and Society* 28, no. 2 (2014).

Stangler, Dane, and Sam Arbesman. "What Does Fortune 500 Turnover Mean?" *Ewing Marion Kauffman Foundation*, 2012. http://www.kauffman.org/~/media/kauffman_org/research%20reports%20and%20cov-ers/2012/06/fortune_500_turnover.pdf.

Stork, Diana, F. Wilson and A.W. Bowles. "The New Workforce Reality: Insights for Today, Implications for Tomorrow." *Simmons School of Management and Bright Horizons Family Solutions*, 2005.

Sue, Derald Wing. *Microaggressions in Everyday Life: Race, Gender, and Sexual Orientation*. New Jersey: John Wiley and Sons, 2010.

Waller, Nikki, and Joann S. Lublin. "What's Holding Women Back in the Workplace?" *Wall Street Journal*, September 30, 2015. https://www.wsj.com/articles/whats-holding-women-back-in-the-work-place-1443600242.

Ward, Gregg. "What Straight, White Guys Don't Get About Diversity and Why." *The Multicultural Advantage*. Accessed May 2, 2017. http://www.multiculturaladvantage.com/recruit/diversity/white-men-diversity/What-Straight-White-Guys-Do-Not-Get-About-Diversity-and-Why.asp.

The White House Project. *The White House Project: Benchmarking Women's Leadership*, 2009. https://www.in.gov/icw/files/benchmark_wom_leadership.pdf.

Wikipedia contributors. "Four Stages of Competence." *Wikipedia*. Accessed May 2, 2017. https://en.wikipedia.org/wiki/Four_stages_of_competence.

Wikipedia contributors. "Katherine Johnson." *Wikipedia*. Accessed May 4, 2017. https://en.wikipedia.org/w/index.php?title=Katherine_Johnson&oldid=778521976.

Wikipedia contributors. "White Privilege." *Wikipedia*. Accessed May 4, 2017. https://en.wikipedia.org/wiki/White_privilege#Definition.

Wise, Tim. "Is Sisterhood Conditional?: White Women and the Rollback of Affirmative Action." *Timwise.org*, September 23, 1998. http://www.timwise.

org/1998/09/is-sisterhood-conditional-white-women-and-the-rollback-of-affirmative-action/.

World Economic Forum. *Gender Equality Is Sliding Backwards, Finds Our Global Report*, 2016. https://www.weforum.org/agenda/2016/10/gender-gap-report-2016-equality-sliding-backwards/.

World Health Organization. *World Malaria Report 2014*, 2014. http://www.who.int/malaria/publications/world_malaria_report_2014/en/.

Yang, Jenny. "Job Discrimination Still a Challenge." Editorial. *Miami Herald* (Miami, FL), July 1, 2015.

Yoshino, Kenji. *Covering: The Hidden Assault on Our Civil Rights*. New York: Random House, 2006.

Zander, Rosamund Stone, and Benjamin Zander, *The Art of Possibility*. New York: Penguin Books, 2000.

Zillman, Claire. "Ruth Bader Ginsburg Used This Simple Trick to Cut Down on 'Manterrupting.'" *Fortune Magazine*, April 2017. http://fortune.com/2017/04/06/ruth-bader-ginsburg-supreme-court-advice-interrupting/.

89936956R00161

Made in the USA
Middletown, DE
20 September 2018